Out On The Limbs

Searching For Answers
In The Family Tree

Sean M. Teaford

authorHOUSE®

AuthorHouse™
1663 Liberty Drive
Bloomington, IN 47403
www.authorhouse.com
Phone: 1 (800) 839-8640

Interior Graphics/Art Credit: Sean M. Teaford

Published by AuthorHouse   02/26/2016

ISBN: 978-1-5049-8105-7 (sc)
ISBN: 978-1-5049-8106-4 (e)

Library of Congress Control Number: 2016902900

Print information available on the last page.

This book is printed on acid-free paper.

For my son – this is at least part of your family history.

Acknowledgements

Many of us have taken up genealogy to learn more about our families and, subsequently, about ourselves. Along the way there are many people who support us in this endeavor. For me, this work would not have been possible without the previous family research by Nellie Teaford Wood, Cecile Teaford Miller, Harry (Ike) Teaford, Dixie Teaford, and Carolyn Hoagland. Additionally, many of the documents, particularly pictures, which I have been able to obtain have come from many of the aforementioned people as well as Janet Spanier, L. Bruce Johnson, and my parents, John and Betsy Teaford.

While many have contributed photos and documents throughout this research process, the support that I have received from family, friends, and the genealogy community has been tremendous. Not only have they encouraged me to keep pursuing information despite the brick walls that have been encountered but they have also provided me with the guidance, tips, and leads that have been invaluable to this ongoing project.

Thank you all for your contributions to this endeavor as well as to those who have read these essays and offered their support when they were originally posted on my blog, Time To Keep It Simple.

Other Works By Sean M. Teaford

Teaching A Stone To Talk: Nature Poems (Bending Tree Press, 2003)

Kaddish Diary (Pudding House Publications, 2005)

Paintings In Under A Thousand Words: Nature Poems (Author House, 2016)

What Was Not Said: Echoes From The Holocaust (Author House, 2016)

The Good, The Bad, And The Adorable: My First Year As A Father (Author House, 2016)

Contents

Questions and Connections

Reunion Memories

A Genealogist's Perspective

Introduction

When I first started writing about genealogy on my blog the posts were few and far between. However, since my son was born I have become more diligent in my research with the hope of providing him with as complete a family history as possible. These essays are just the beginning.

The genealogy essays in this collection offer a cross section of topics including recent additions to my family tree, interesting resources or programs, and discoveries that give greater depth to the lives of my ancestors. This past year I had to make a couple of updates to my tree. One that I had been dreading for months and the other that I have been looking forward to for nine months. Two changes that clearly demonstrate the dichotomy of the basic information that we all encounter as we trace our roots... birth and death.

Both of these additions of information were almost surreal after having spent so much time digging through centuries of family history and piles of ancestral records. It was a change in perception as I would previously dig through pages and pages just trying to find out when someone died but now, having experienced that last moment, it was not something that brought me any closure whatsoever and by doing so, I think back to all the other times that I had to record that information for other loved ones in my tree.

From one unique experience to another. There are names that I see over and over again on both sides of my family and by adding my son's leaf, one of those names repeats itself for another generation. The name we chose, especially the spelling, was a means to connect my tree and my wife's tree. Our son's name adds to that bond between our deeply rooted family histories.

While he certainly doesn't comprehend any of this now, I look forward to the day when we can introduce our son to his entire family and the history that his name carries with it. Between the two trees, there is a complex history spanning much of the world. My family touches on many areas and different cultures and my wife's family covers a completely different geography and part of world history.

Each leaf has a little more to add to the family history just as each piece of fall foliage adds to the autumnal landscape. All different trees offering a different variety of colors but working in unison to tell the same story. That is what our son has to look forward to and what I am looking forward to sharing with our son.

Profiles and Discoveries

At the State House at Philadelphia
Saturday 27th October 1764

Present
Thomas Willing Esquire

The Foreigners whose names are underwritten imported in the Ship
Polly Ralph Forster from Rotterdam, last from Cowes, did this day
take and subscribe the usual Qualifications
(Messrs Willing & Morris)

Answering An Unknown Number

It grazed my mind that I should call a couple of the places I sent emails to just before the holidays regarding membership. I reached out because in order to become a member of these heritage based organizations you need to prove your lineage as well as have a member sponsor your application. However, like so many thoughts in the midst of a hectic day, it quickly evaporated in the bitterly cold dry air not to touch upon the gray matter for the remainder of the working hours. At least that is what I thought....

Toward the end of the day my phone began to ring as I was waiting for my email to refresh on the screen. Not recognizing the number in question, I swiped my finger across the screen and answered in a usual authoritative business-like manner. While the accent caught me off guard, I quickly realized that one of the tasks forgotten during the early part of the work day was about to take care of itself. And so our conversation began.

While trying to rekindle the genealogy research that has been put on hold in recent months (upon months) I began looking for different groups and heritage societies in the area where I might be able to, at a minimum, learn a little bit more about the culture in the deep and distant past of my family (most of our long standing heritage could easily be described simply as American). The two dominant cultures in my family histories (yes, there are numerous blood lines, stories, and histories) are of German and Irish origin with Germany having a substantial percentage lead. Honestly not knowing much about either I looked for different groups where I may learn a little more. That led me to the Irish Society and the German Society of Pennsylvania (both located in Philadelphia). Because you need a member to sponsor you for each I sent out emails in late December.

Today, when I answered the phone, I knew what the call was about as soon as I heard the thin German accent. It was an interesting conversation because this was a man I had never met before but you could tell in our dialog that we shared a common interest and at some level an ancestral bond. Making the connection even stronger is the fact that the Society was founded about two months after Jacob Duffordt arrived in Philadelphia aboard the Hero on the 27th of October 1764. My family and this proud society share the same anniversary and we will both be celebrating 250 years.

While there are blood lines that I can trace further back in this land and even a few that were here since before the colonies were even a consideration, the celebration of your surname, your family name, does add a tremendous amount of appreciation, pride, and humility. I am proud to be a very small part in the story of my family and I am hoping to bring things around full circle by honoring our heritage and appreciating a bit of the culture we carried with us on that prolonged and exhausting journey across the ocean from Rotterdam to Philadelphia. Just goes to show that sometimes you have to take a step back or return to the beginning in order to keep moving forward.

Revolutionary Resources

As I have peered through the leaves in my family tree and followed branches out to their blooming tips I have come across a number of lines that can be traced back to the time of the American Revolution. Whenever I discover and ancestor that lived in the United States during this time period there are a few resources that I turn to in order to find out if there is any record of their participation in the war. While these resources don't guarantee an answer (there are a lot of documents that have not been digitally archived at this point), it does offer a convenient starting place.

The first site that I browse is the one where I keep my tree, ancestry.com, which has added a number of relevant documents lately. I first look to find any source material that may be available with particular attention paid to the SAR applications that come up in searches. Whether I find something or not I next browse the trees of other members to see if they either have the information that I couldn't previously find or if they have any additional information that adds to the developing story. While there have been occasions when the family history has already begun to unfold, there have been many instances when nothing has come about from this primary search.

Whether I am already working with results or not, I next turn to another favorite source, the DAR patriot database. This site offers another layer of research as by inputting the name of the ancestor in question, you can find all applications that have been submitted using that ancestor as their proof of ties to the American Revolution. There have been a few occasions when nothing has come up on ancestry.com but numerous applications appeared in the DAR database.

If you find a match here you can request a copy of the application which provides additional information including the sources used to verify each generation and the patriotic service. While it does cost $10 per record, it is a wealth of information that can save you a lot of time. Also worth noting is that SAR and DAR applications can be referenced in your own application to these respective organizations... this reduces the burden of proof down to that of the generations needed in order to trace back to an overlapping ancestor on an existing application of a member.

The last place that I search for information is on fold3.com. While this can be utilized early on I have found that without a membership there can be too many frustrations that prevent me from verifying or disproving service. However, there are occasions when access is free to certain collections (last month was the Civil War while this month is WWII). When access to Revolutionary War documents is free for a certain period, this is a tool that I will employ earlier in the process either prior to or after an ancestry.com search. Once I finish this stage of the process there is a fairly certain answer resulting from my efforts as to whether an ancestor participated in the Revolution. Surprisingly, more often than not, I have been able to find the sources to confirm their participation.

Of course, there are other sources that sometimes provide additional insights. There have been a few instances when the obituaries found on geneaologybank.com have led to the discovery of revolutionary ancestors. This has also been a resource to confirm based on newspaper articles. However, keep in mind that this is just one process for one period in history. It is the method that has worked best for me and has proven to be the most efficient means to finding the answers that I am looking for. It may not work for everyone but it may be useful to some.

Augusta County State of Virginia

I do hereby Certify that I have Received of
Thomas Tate Four hundred and fourteen pounds of Good flour at fifty pounds per
hundred weight payable at the Treasury of Virginia within Six months
from this Date with an interest six per centum thereon agreeable to late
Act of General assembly for procuring a supply of Provisions for the
use of the army Given under my hand this twenty fifth day of October
one thousand eleven hundred and Eighty

414 £3:2:2   John Moffet Col

Augusta county virginia

I do hereby certify that
Thomas Tate is entitled to Receive eighty four
pounds for Seven Bushel of Rye Payable at the
Treasury of Virginia within Six months from the
date agreeable to an act of General Assembly for
Procuring a Supply of Provision and other necessaries
for the use of the Army given under my hand this
7th day of November 1780

7 bus: Rye a 3/ £1:1 :   Joseph Bell Co. Comr
(furnished Comr of Prov. Laws in Augusta)
Allow'd at 2/6 per Bushel

Augusta County State of Virginia

I do hereby Certify that I have Rec'd of
Jacob Teaford fifty five pounds of Good flour at fifty
pounds per hundred weight payable at the treasury
of Virginia within six months from this date with
an interest of six per centum thereon agreeable to a late
act of General assembly for procuring a supply of provisions
and other necessaries for the use of the army Given
under my hand this Seventh day of December one thousand
seven hundred and Eighty   John Moff.D Col L
55 7 Decr 80

Six Degrees of Revolution

One of my longstanding annual goals was to finally complete my Sons of the American Revolution application. Well, after sifting through the hundreds of documents on my computer, I had made significant progress. So far, I have found six ancestors who participated in the war effort to support the Continental Army.

However, I can only sufficiently support through documentation one of the lines. This line is that of John Redcross who, according to records, fought both in the 2ndVirginia Regiment and the Amherst County Militia. This is not particularly uncommon for many of the Native Americans in the area as they were valued contributors to the cause due to their unparalleled knowledge of the mountains. Here is the line that connects me to the Revolution (records used to prove the lines are mentioned after the ancestor):

JOHN REDCROSS

- ME – Birth Certificate
- FATHER – Marriage License and Birth Certificate
  - Vietnam War – Military Records
- Percy Davis Teaford (1918 – 1985) – Marriage License, Birth Certificate, Census Records, Family Interviews
  - World War II – Military Records
- Nettie Caldwell Love (1897 – 1972) – Death Record, Census Records, Family Interviews, Marriage Records
- Laura Belle Redcross / Cross (1862 – 1938) – Census Records, Family Interviews
  - Last Full Blood Monacan Indian in this line.
- Paulus E. Redcross / Redcrop (1828 – 1914) – Census Records, DAR Application of Shelby Jean Wood Penn

- John Redcross (1768 – 1861) – Birth Record, Marriage Record, Census Records, DAR Application of Shelby Jean Wood Penn
- John Redcross (1740 – 1800) – Virginia Tax List Record of 1793, DAR Application of Shelby Jean Wood Penn
  - 2nd Virginia Regiment (1779) and Amherst County Militia (1781) – Muster Roll, Records of Virginia Militia Members during 1781.
  - Monacan Indian Chief – Founding Father of the Modern Monacan Nation. Burial on Bear Mountain in Virginia.

Not all men were able to fight in the revolution; some did what they could to contribute to the cause monetarily and through the sale of goods. This was an important demonstration of patriotism and support shown by many men who were either physically unable to fight or they simply had to do what they could to support and protect their families from home. Jacob Düffordt was one of those men. Here is the line that is one step away from being fully substantiated:

JACOB DÜFFORDT

- ME – Birth Certificate
- FATHER – Marriage License and Birth Certificate
  - Vietnam War – Military Records
- Percy Davis Teaford (1918 – 1985) – Marriage License, Birth Certificate, Census Records, Family Interviews
  - World War II – Military Records
- Harry Gilmore Teaford (1895 – 1963) – Marriage License, Birth Certificate, Census Records, Family Interviews
- Roy / Rolly Harrison Teaford (1857 – 1914) – Marriage License, Birth Certificate, Census Records
- John Wesley Teaford (1837 – 1909) – Marriage License, Birth Certificate, Census Records
  - Civil War – Pension Records and Muster Roles
- Jacob Teaford (1790 – 1877) – Marriage License, Birth Certificate, Census Records

- o War of 1812 – Pension Papers
- Jacob Teaford / Düfford (1768 – 1840) – Census Records, Wills, Deeds, Court Records, Engagement Records
- Jacob Düffordt (1734 – 1800) – Deeds, Will, Census Records
  - o Donated 55 pounds of flour to the Continental Army of Virginia (1784) – Receipt from Continental Army
  - o Arrived in Philadelphia on 27 October 1764 on the Hero from a German enclave in the Alsace – Lorraine region of France (considered a German immigrant) – Ship Manifest

John Jacob Myers is the first of the Pennsylvania contributors that I came across. From immigration to independence, here was a full life lived. I am further still from providing documented support throughout this line:

JOHN JACOB MYERS

- ME – Birth Certificate
- FATHER – Marriage License and Birth Certificate
  - o Vietnam War – Military Records
- Isabelle Ardis Hallman (1920 – 1980) – Birth Record, Death Record, Marriage License, Census Records, Family Interviews.
- Sarah Mabel Ardis (1899 – 1982) – Birth Record, Death Record, Marriage Record, Census Records, Family Interviews.
- Sarah Hansell Myers (1874 – 1932) – Birth Record, Death Record, Marriage Record, Census Records.
- Henry Levi Myers Jr. (1841 – 1941) – Birth Record, Death Record, Census Records.
- Henry Levi Myers Sr. (1809 – 1893) – Birth Record, Death Record, Marriage Record, Census Records.
- Isaac Myers (1784 – 1867) – Birth Record, Death Record, Marriage Record, Census Records.
- John Heinrich Myers (1765 – 1837) – Birth Record, Death Record, Marriage Record, Census Records, Land Grant.
- John Jacob Myers (1732 – 1808) – Birth Record, Death Record, Marriage Record, Census Records, Naturalization Papers.

- ○ 6th Pennsylvania Battalion out of Lancaster – Muster Rolls, Veterans Burial Card.
- ○ Arrived in approximately 1760 from Westphalia, Germany – Naturalization Papers.

Now we come to the only ancestor I could find up to this point that, so aptly put by President Lincoln 87 years later, "gave the last full measure of devotion." Rufus Cone wasn't able to fully embrace independence. In fact, he spent his final moments stripped of his freedom and taken from his newly declared country. While the "proof" may not be there yet, the family connection is strong.

RUFUS CONE

- ME – Birth Certificate
- FATHER – Marriage License and Birth Certificate
  - ○ Vietnam War – Military Records
- Isabel Ardis Hallman (1920 – 1980) – Birth Record, Death Record, Marriage License, Census Records, Family Interviews.
- Sarah Mabel Ardis (1899 – 1982) – Birth Record, Death Record, Marriage Record, Census Records, Family Interviews.
- Sarah Hansell Myers (1874 – 1932) – Birth Record, Death Record, Marriage Record, Census Records.
- Lizzie F. Hansell (1848 – 1879) – Death Record, Census Records.
- Margaret Cone (1825 – 1899) – Census Records.
- Rufus Cone (1784 – 1846) – Census Records, SAR Application of Charles George Leeper
- Azel Cone (1763 – 1820) – Birth Record, Census Records, SAR Application of Charles George Leeper
- Rufus Cone (1737 – 1776) – Census Records, SAR Application of Charles George Leeper
  - ○ 7th and 17th Connecticut Regiments.
  - ○ Taken prisoner at the Battle of Long Island 27 August 1776.
  - ○ Died aboard British prisoner ship.

Someone had to be the politician in the family and in mine it was John Fulton. Another immigrant to the colonies, both John and his son served in the Revolution. While the ender was representing the people in a government defying the political odds, his son was in the field fighting for an as of yet unknown Pennsylvania regiment. While there is still much work to be done on this line my current research has resulted in the fascinating lineage listed below.

JOHN FULTON

- ME – Birth Certificate
- MOTHER – Marriage License, Birth Certificate.
- William Reuben McKannan (1914 – 1981) – Marriage License, Birth Certificate, Census Records, Masonic Record, Family Interviews, Draft Registration Card, Family Albums.
- Helen Walker Fulton (1892 – 1922) – Marriage Record, Birth Record, Death Record, Census Records.
- William Harvey Fulton (1858 – 1930) – Census Records.
- James H. Fulton (1829 – 1894) – Census Records, Tombstone, Pension Papers, Draft Cards.
  - o Civil War – Pension Papers, Muster Rolls.
- Hugh Fulton (1784 – 1843) – Census Records, Death Record, Marriage Record.
- John Fulton Jr. (1755 – 1808) – Census Records, Tombstone, Veterans Records.
  - o Unknown Pennsylvania Regiment
- John Fulton Sr. (1713 – 1796) – Census Records, County Documents, SAR Application of Alfred Miller Fulton.
  - o Member of the Pennsylvania General Assembly (1776 – 1779) from Chester County – County Documents, SAR Application of Alfred Miller Fulton.
  - o Arrived in 1762 from Scotland and settled near Oxford, Chester County, Pennsylvania – Census Records, SAR Application of Alfred Miller Fulton.

The last of the connections I have been able to uncover is that of Samuel Dickey Jr. A first generation American, it has been said that he was among the men who crossed the Delaware River in December 1776 under the command of General George Washington. Currently this is hearsay but it will be an adventure either proving of disproving it.

SAMUEL DICKEY JR.

- ME – Birth Certificate
- MOTHER – Marriage License, Birth Certificate.
- William Reuben McKannan (1914 – 1981) – Marriage License, Birth Certificate, Census Records, Masonic Record, Family Interviews, Draft Registration Card, Family Albums.
- Helen Walker Fulton (1892 – 1922) – Marriage Record, Birth Record, Death Record, Census Records.
- William Harvey Fulton (1858 – 1930) – Census Records.
- James H. Fulton (1829 – 1894) – Census Records, Tombstone, Pension Papers, Draft Cards.
  - Civil War – Pension Papers, Muster Rolls.
- Hugh Fulton (1784 – 1843) – Census Records, Death Record, Marriage Record.
- Jane Dickey (1765 – 1796) – Census Records, Tombstone.
- Samuel Dickey Jr. (1730 – 1795) – Census Records, Tombstone, Chester County Historical Marker, Veterans Index.
  - Served under General Washington during the Crossing of the Delaware River on 25-26 December 1776 – Revolutionary War Rolls, Veterans Index.
- Samuel Dickey Sr. (1708 – 1778) – Census Records, County Records.
  - Arrived in 1730 from Ireland and settled near Oxford, Chester County, Pennsylvania.

Those are my six degrees of Revolution (as of right now). Obviously, I will continue to research each of these ancestors in the hope of building support for these lines. Maybe all will be proven; maybe only one or two more; maybe I will make more connections; maybe I will only be able to prove the current definitive line. Who knows but I am going to keep learning about the history of my family and, therefore, the history of this country.

Do you have a genealogical connection to the Revolution? Maybe not, maybe your family's ties to independence came later. Either way we are all a part of this country and we are all united by the rights and freedoms fought for during that time. What is your family's story?

*Please note that since this post was originally written, there have been a few of the aforementioned lines disproven and even more documented in the family.

Pay Roll of Captain William Longs Company of the 2 Virg^a State Regiment Commanded by Col^o Brent for Septr 1779

218

	Names	Rank	Months	[illegible]	Subsistence	Sum in Dollars	Remarks
	William Long	Capt	1	40	200	240	
	John Hardyman	Lieut	1	26⅔	100	126⅔	
1	Gray Samuel	Ser^t	1	10	10	20	
2	Augustine Weedon	d^o	1	—	—	20	
3	John Cason	d^o	—	—	—	20	
1	Ephraim Lawson	Corp^l	1	7⅓	10	17⅓	
2	James Poland	d^o	—	—	—	17⅓	
3	James [illegible]	d^o	—	—	—	17⅓	
1	Obediah Bowler	Drum^r	1	7⅓	10	17⅓	
2	Samuel Lucas	Fifer d^o	—	—	—	17⅓	
1	John Baker	Priv^t	1	6⅔	10	16⅔	
2	James Taylor	d^o	—	—	—	16⅔	
3	Ambrose Roberts	—	—	—	—	16⅔	
4	Francis Arnold	—	—	—	—	16⅔	
5	Charles Hill	—	—	—	—	16⅔	
6	Jesse Jones	—	—	—	—	16⅔	
7	William Hill	—	—	—	—	16⅔	
8	[illegible] Bowler	—	—	—	—	16⅔	
9	Moses Green	—	3	6⅔	10⅔	34⅔	Omitted in July & August Pay Rolls
10	William Anderson	—	1	—	—	16⅔	
11	Richard Mott	—	—	—	—	16⅔	
12	Francis Murry	—	—	—	—	16⅔	
13	John Major	—	—	—	—	16⅔	
14	Thomas Moore	—	—	—	—	16⅔	
15	Gerrat Commins	—	—	—	—	16⅔	
16	[illegible] Roberts	—	—	—	—	16⅔	
17	John [illegible]	—	—	—	—	16⅔	
18	James [illegible]	—	—	—	—	16⅔	
19	John Mallory	—	—	—	—	16⅔	
20	William Moore	—	—	—	—	16⅔	
21	Larkin Phillips	—	—	—	—	16⅔	
22	James Cason	—	—	—	—	16⅔	
23	William Cason	—	—	—	—	16⅔	
						914⅓	Dollars

SAR Update

As many of you may recall reading, I have been trying to find the time over the past few years to finally sit down, pull together all the documents, and submit my application to the local chapter of the Sons of the American Revolution. Of course, up until last week I hadn't even reached out to the SAR to get additional information so that was the first step that I had to take. So, out of the blue, I looked up the local contact information and gave the chapter a call. After a very nice, informative, and welcoming conversation I received some sound advice as to how I should proceed the most important of which was to start with the ancestor that I can most easily prove.

My goal when I made the call was to get everything pulled together over the next several weeks, two weeks if I was lucky. This seemed to be an agreeable and manageable arrangement for both of us and I was encouraged to attend meetings in the meantime while I was finishing up my application. By the time we ended our conversation I already knew which ancestor made the most sense. While the documents that I have in my possession are not enough for the Monacan Indian Nation, they are more than enough to prove to the SAR that I am a descendant of John Redcross.

Well, somehow I finally found the time to get it done and I was able to submit all 200+ pages to the local chapter for review. This past week has been a time to review the application that I submitted and, surprisingly, a time for the chapter genealogist to condense the documentation down to only the items needed. We really do have more than enough to prove our lineage and, at the same time, not enough. Now we can focus on finding that final piece so that we can submit the same material to the Monacan Nation.

It is a great feeling knowing that this is done and that after this it will be a matter of adding confirmed patriots to the family history. Heeding the advice of the SAR, now I am going to move to the next easiest to prove which happens to be on the other side of my family. While we once thought it impossible, I have been able to trace back my mom's side to the Revolution and have the documentation to support the findings. It is nice to know that basically no matter which family member I am talking to I can help them join the SAR (or DAR).

However, the most important aspect to this whole process for me is that it is a means to verify the research that I have spent the last few years conducting. The more lines I can confirm and revolutionary ancestors I can trace back to, the more information in our tree I will be able to verify. Having had so many questions about the family history growing up, I am looking forward to sharing with the family a history that has been not only researched by certified as being accurate. And, one day, I look forward to sharing this history with my son.

Every Once In A While I Have A N.S. Moment

I have been trying for days to think of a good quote to use this week that sums up an unexpected moment. Finally, early this afternoon it struck me when I found myself saying "No S**t!" when my wife and I were browsing in a small gift shop in Kutztown. I found myself uttering those eloquent words in a haze of disbelief when I came across a postcard. To many it is nothing special, maybe an interesting picture and record of many of the American Indian tribes across North America. But it was a completely different experience for me.

Usually, I wouldn't pay too much attention to such an illustration but, for some reason, I decided to pick it up and take a closer look. What I found had been rare in my genealogical research experience thus far… I found the Monacan name on a map. Even upon a second and third look the name was still there.

As was mentioned in a previous essay, one of my many ancestral lines is that of a Monacan Indian (possibly Chief) by the name of John Redcross. Not much is written or generally known about this Amherst County, Virginia Nation but, slowly, the name and the history is beginning to gain acceptance. Even with my limited knowledge about this particular part of my heritage, I still felt a certain amount of pride when my eyes fell upon those letters.

It's hard to explain but it was an amazing experience to find that one word on a small little souvenir at a tourist stop in Southeastern Pennsylvania. One word with a lot of weight. One Nation scribed in ink. One people recognized in a small but significant way.

Revisiting 1934 And Reversing 'Paper Genocide'

This past week I came across an article published by Michael Melia of the Associated Press that was both encouraging and disappointing. The story talks about the U.S. Interior Department's attempt to overhaul the current rules in place for recognizing American Indian tribes (the draft is currently open for discussion until September 25th). However, by the second sentence, and I guess you could say it's inevitable, the casino card is played as if it is the only reason why tribes desire federal recognition. Here is how the reporter opens the story:

> His tribe once controlled huge swaths of what is now New York and Connecticut, but the shrunken reservation presided over by Alan Russell today hosts little more than four mostly dilapidated homes and a pair of rattlesnake dens.

> The Schaghticoke Indian Tribe leader believes its fortunes may soon be improving. As the U.S. Interior Department overhauls its rules for recognizing American Indian tribes, a nod from the federal government appears within reach, potentially bolstering its claims to surrounding land and opening the door to a tribal-owned casino.

> "It's the future generations we're fighting for," Russell said.

> The rules floated by the Bureau of Indian Affairs, intended to streamline the approval process, are seen by some as lowering the bar through changes such as one requiring that tribes demonstrate political continuity since 1934 and not "first contact" with European settlers. Across the country, the push is setting up battles with host communities and already recognized tribes who fear upheaval.

As a writer, I understand that you are trying to give the story a visual reference but the true basis of this argument can't be in the material gains that potential changes could provide. The real reason is a recognized identity which has been withheld from countless people across the nation. The proposed changes recognize the governmental and regional neglect that has remained prevalent since this nation's founding.

People who were marginalized and forced from their home and their land, encouraged to disband and sever ties with their native roots and join 'the civilized world' face a daunting task in establishing the existence of their own families across generations let alone the continuous continuity of their tribe. This is why the change in definition is needed. This is why the simple line in the "Procedures For Establishing That An American Indian Group Exists As An Indian Tribe" carries such great weight and the balance of that weight needs to be shifted to accommodate the historical burdens of segregation and persecution. Seeing this seemingly simple edit brings a touch of hopeful sweetness to the bitterness that has soured numerous attempts to be recognized. "Continuously or continuous means extending from ~~first sustained contact with non-Indians throughout the group's history~~ 1934 to the present substantially without interruption."

It is a change that can help heal the history in a place such as Virginia where anti-Semitism and "The Racial Integrity Act" tried to erase not just the present American Indian population but the identities of Indian ancestors as well. It is a means to finally put an end to the work of Virginia's longtime registrar at the commonwealth's Bureau of Vital Statistics, Dr. Walter Ashby Plecker who wrote "...Like rats when you are not watching, [they] have been 'sneaking' in their birth certificates through their own midwives, giving either Indian or white racial classification."

Supported by previous actions by Virginia's government to force American Indians to register as free blacks in the 1850's and 1860's, Plecker's eugenics based campaign continued to taint the identities of Indian children throughout the 20th century. While Virginia repealed its racial definition and segregation laws in 1975 it was still a time consuming and emotionally draining process for families to appeal decisions made at birth which misidentified their children robbing them of their ancestry. Further hindering federal recognition efforts is the fact that state recognition of Virginia based tribes did not come into existence until the 1980's when only eight remained (including the Monacan Nation).

Contrary to what many people in opposition of this amendment have decried, this is not a matter of land or casinos; this is about identity and ensuring the historical integrity of American Indian tribes survives. It is about recognition and resurrecting what was once excised from the historical record. It is an act that would allow us to say "We Exist!"

Land

Land is an important part of family history. It gives us the connection to previous generations, decades, centuries, and sometimes millennia after the lives of our ancestors. Knowing where we come from and finding those roots has always been something that has been of particular interest to me. This is part of what has driven me in recent years to find that land of our own where my wife and I can raise our family... and actual place, a piece of this earth, that we own. This was also important to the first generation of my family in the late 18th century.

```
          GIVEN at my Office in Frederick County under my Hand and Seal
          Dated the Twenty third Day of April 1778
                                                    Fairfax  April 23,
    (.                                                         1778
         Casper Rinker Deed for 427
      C    in Fredrick County                B Mastin

              The Right Honorable Thomas Lord Fairfax Baron of Cameron in that
    part of Great Britain called Scotland Properitor of the Northern Neck of
    Virginia to all to whom this present writing shall come sends Greetings and
    know up that for good caoses for and in consideration of the composition to
    me paid and for the annual Rent herein after received I have given granted
    and confirmed and by these presents for me my Heirs and Assigns do give grant
    and confirm unto Jacob Defort of Shanandoah County a certain tract of waste
    and ungranted land in the said County bounded as by a survey thereof made
    by John Hough and Beginning at 3 chestnut oaks corner to George Coffield and
    extending thence with his line S45E Two hundred and forty poles to 3 pines
    and a white oak corner to the said Coffield and Valentine Coffield,then with
    his line S48W88 poles to several marked white oak saplings corner to the
    said Coffield and in a line of Cagale Fler.Then with Fler's line N27N39 poles
    to 2 white oaks and a gum corner to the said Fler.Then with another of his
    lines S65W 94 poles to 2 white oaks standing in Fler's line-then N45W180 pole
    to a white oak near the 3 mile mountain-then N7W64 poles to 2 pines on the
    side of a hill.Then N38W60 poles to a pine on the side of the said mountain
    and then S88E172 poles to the beginning containing two hundred and sixty-eigh
    acres and together with all rights.Members and appertenances there unto belon
    ging Bayal Mines excepted and a full third part of all lead,copper,tin coats,
    from mine and iron ore that shall be found therein-To have and to hold the
    (            said 268 acres of land together with all Rights Profits and Benefits to
              the same belonging or in anywise appertaining except before excepted and
    to whom the said Jacob Defort his heirs and assigns forever and he the said
    Jacob Defort his heirs and assigns yielding and paying to me my heirs and
    assigns to any certainic attorney or attornies agent or agents or to the
    certainic attorney or attornies of my heirs or assigns properietors of the
    said Northern Neck yearly and every year on the feast Day of St Michael
    the Archangel the fee rent of one Shilling Sterling money for every fifty
    acres of land hereby granted and proportionably for a greater or lesser Qu
    antity and provided that if said Jacob Defort his heirs and assigns shall
    not pay the said reserved annual rent aforesaid so that the same or any part
    therefor shall be behind and unpaid by the space of two whole years after
    the same shall become due,legally demanded that then it shall and maybe law
    ful for me my heirs and assigns properietors as aforesaid my or their cert-
    ainic attorney or attornies agent or agents into the above granted promises
    to renter and hold the same so as if this grant had never been given at my
    Office in Frederick County,under my Hand and Seal dated the Twenty-fourth
    Day of April 1778  -

         Jacob Defort's Deed for 268
         Acres in Shanandoah County              Fairfax
```

From Nellie Teaford Wood's book which is included on the family website:

In 1780 Jacob Düfford bought his first farm in Augusta County at the foot of Sugar Loaf Mountain, a small round hill on property now part of Silverbrook Farms. With his wife Christenah and six children he came from Shenandoah County, where he had resided since 1774 on land in the Fairfax Grant.

Düfford had arrived in Philadelphia on the ship Hero on 27 October 1764, but his origin has eluded researchers. That he spoke and read and wrote German is established by his signatures in Philadelphia and in October 1792 in Virginia. He joined 193 residents in petitioning the Virginia General Assembly, citing their unacquaintance with the English "language" to publish laws in German so that "they may more cheerfully comply" because they have "always contributed their part of the support of government."

Virginia State claims show that he, along with other "Augusta Germans," did his part by furnishing flour for the Revolutionary army in 1780.

. . .

The immigrant Jacob died intestate in 1801, owning three farms. The papers settling the estate in Augusta County Courthouse offer a wealth of genealogical and historical information.

We didn't have much when came to this country, colony actually, but we worked and slowly accumulated land. This was particularly important during this time in history as only landowners could vote and have any say in such petitions as the one to which he affixed his name in 1792. In the end, over the course of his life, Jacob had acquired over 200 acres in Augusta County. Makes my nearly 3 acres, purchased 235 years after Jacob bought his first farm, seem almost inconsequential in comparison.

In the years since that first generation, the family has seen land come and go in the family but those original farms, while not in the family, still exist. They still remain as a connection to our past regardless of who currently holds the deed. Being able to go down to Virginia, gather with those who have this same connection, and enjoy the area where we know our family has been for hundreds of years is something that we were able to enjoy over the summer and an experience I look forward to revisiting many times over in the future.

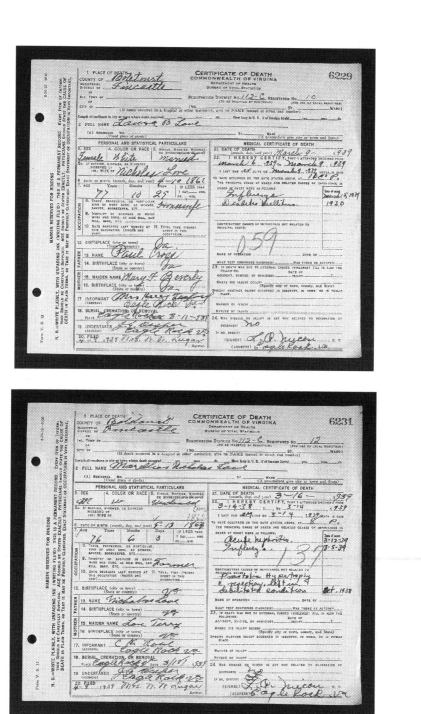

New/Old Records On Ancestry

While I would like to be on the site more often, I am only occasionally able to check Ancestry.com for updates to the various databases that are available online. Recently, I have had less time than usual to browse the site but was able to do so today. There are always new data sources and updates made but, especially lately, few have caught my attention like the ones I found today.

This past week, birth, marriage, and death records from Virginia were posted. While the date range is limited and they are by no means comprehensive collections, I was still able to find some new records as well as digital copies of records that I haven't had the chance to upload. While the latter may not be new information, given the current disarray of my office, this was a welcomed discovery.

With these databases now available, I was able to explore a little more and find a few of the missing documents that I had been wanting to find including my great grandfathers birth certificate (albeit a registration from 1958), my great great grandfathers death certificate (I had found this information listed but was unable until now to find the actual record), the death certificate for my three times great grandfather, and the elusive Love and Redcross death certificates which I got copies of last summer but are sitting in a box next to my desk. It is interesting to go through these documents and confirm the parents (especially the mother's surname)... I really didn't expect to see Nicholas' mother listed as a Terry. However, what was particularly striking was the fact that Laura and Nicholas Love's death certificates were only a number apart from one another with them passing away only days apart from influenza (with some other contributing factors). It was just sad to see Nicholas listed as a widower when you know that Laura died only a few days prior.

Just like when the Pennsylvania records became available, I keep searching my family tree to find those that fit into the time frame. There are a few that I have been unable to find as the rural records are a little slower when it comes to digitization and there are also the ancestors who died just before the time frame of data available. Those are usually the ones that the parents' names need to be confirmed. Also an interesting means of confirmation with these documents is that it tells you not only where they have been buried but also who the informant was at the time of death or who witnessed the birth as in the case of my great grandfather.

Such is the ebb and flow of ancestry when the new sources are added followed by an extended wait and then more databases are added that are pertinent to your family research. In between is the time for digging, organizing, and finding all the more obscure sources and documents which are usually still exclusively in the physical (not digital) world. It is this back and forth multi-source process that continues to provide the results.

Finding Life In Death

Every so often I log on to Ancestry.com to check and see if there are any leaves shaking on the tree. For those of you unfamiliar with the site, this means that there is new information or documents available for review. It doesn't necessarily mean that the information is correct or adds color to that particular ancestor but there are times when interesting discoveries are made. However, I learned early on that you can't simply rely on the quivering foliage so, when I have a few minutes here and there, I do a general search of the site to try and find other information (especially when the spelling of the surname is a little different or flat out incorrect).

This week I have noticed that a lot of the Pennsylvania Death Certificates are now listed. I don't know when they were digitized but I am just noticing them now. While the time frame is a bit of a hindrance (currently only 1906-1940 certificates are listed) there are still plenty of documents that I have been finding. Everything from the tragic deaths of children to the inevitable passing of aged ancestors, the causes run the gamut. These are a great source of information not just about the departure of a relative but they can, most of the time, also be a great way to confirm or correct other generations on your tree… sometimes, like a document I sent to my wife, they can provide the names of the parents which was previously unknown information.

As for my tree, it has been a means of correction and confirmation. The death certificate above lists both parents including the mother's maiden name which is different from that which I previously had listed on my family tree. And it is not a simple adjustment in the spelling… Davenport is nowhere close to Hansel. This doesn't mean that I will be correcting it right away but it gives pause to continuing work on that particular branch. Obviously, some more work and verification needs to be done before I change or continue with the tree as is.

These documents are also a means to confirm residence, family health problems (that may have made it across the generations), longevity, and occupation. Sometimes it is a matter of confirming many of those things at the same time. One such document added to the long list of railroad workers in my family while another verified the service of my great great grandfather in the Philadelphia Police Department… I just didn't realize that he spent 54 years on the force.

In the end, while the primary purpose of these documents was to record the death of the family member, there is more life in them than some people realize… definitely more than what can be found in most census records. All of the information is there and it could lead to some interesting discoveries and answer questions or doubts that you may have had about your family. Just goes to show that we need to read the documents rather than just attaching them to an ancestor.

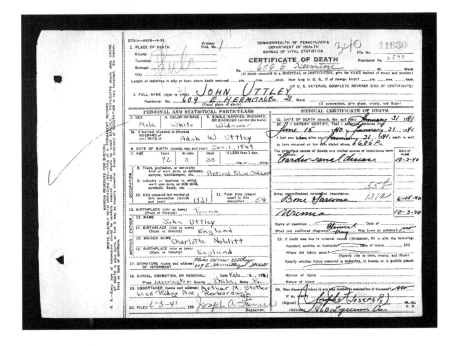

A Second Marriage

On June 21, 1892, my great great grandfather, Roy Teaford, married for the second time to Sally Bette Clapsaddle. Roy, who can also be found under many other names, had lost his first wife, Mildred McNulty, earlier in the year and had employed Sally to care for his three young children. It is unclear exactly how the relationship developed over the months but, by summer, the two married and soon after began having children of their own. This included my great grandfather, Harry Gilmore Teaford, who was born just over three years after they first married on September 28, 1895.

Both Roy and Sally had deep roots in Virginia with both families predating the Revolutionary War. Roy had spent his life to that point laying track for the railroads through the Appalachian Mountains while Sally, 13 years his junior, was only just beginning her life beyond the walls of her childhood home. Roy came from a long line of farmers, from his great great grandfather Jacob Teaford who arrived in the colonies on October 27, 1764 to his grandfather, Jacob Teaford, who served in the War of 1812 and his father, John Wesley Teaford, who was the first to move the family out of Augusta County.

Sally's family was long a mystery to me but the lines that have been explored in recent years are rather fascinating. Sally's parents, George William Clapsaddle and Margaret Ann Bowyer, married shortly after George returned from serving in the Confederate Army during the Civil War and settled in Botetourt County. Ironically, both of her parent's families trace their roots back to Pennsylvania having migrated down to Virginia around the same time that Roy's family was arriving on the continent with both the Clapsaddle and Bowyer families intermarrying throughout the 19th century and during parts of both the 18th and 20th centuries. Many of these records can be found in "The Related Families of Botetourt County, Virginia".

When all the other lines from both Roy and Sally's families are taken into consideration it is astounding how far the family tree stretches throughout Virginia as well as many of the other colonies. Some of those surnames include Cook, Bailey, Riggins, Pemberton, Stinson, Belcher, Snider, Wilfong, Veitheim, Stever, Brown, Schmucker, Steel, Hester, Rinehart, Mankey, Niday and Caldwell. Of course, there are alternate spellings for just about each one as well. Basically, if you scan the pages of the history books you are bound to find at least one of these surnames somewhere in the pages. All of these names tracing back to two people, my great great grandparents, Roy Teaford and Sally Clapsaddle.

Virginia Cemeteries

A while back I drove around to the some of the local cemeteries to find some family members that have been forgotten as well as to visit some that we just hadn't seen in a while. Actually, it was the first time that I can remember visiting any of them. It is with this trip still fresh in my mind (even two years later) that I decided to do the same thing, this time in Virginia.

The day after the reunion, we made our way to Eagle Rock and explored the place where my family once lived. After walking around the small town for a little while, we took my great uncle up on his offer to lead us to one of the cemeteries in the area. After a few turns down gravel roads and a couple of stops to regroup and figure out where we were going we finally made it to Shiloh Cemetery. Here we found my three times great grandmother, Francis Cross / Redcross (Beverly) resting beside her son as well as one of her daughters, Mary Jane Duke (Redcross), and her family just a few yards away.

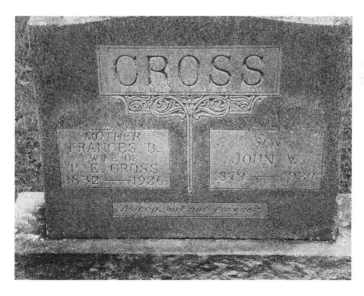

Unfortunately, we are still unable to find my three times great grandfather, Paulus Redcross, who passed long before his wife. After Shiloh we were on our own but fortunately, this time, knew exactly where we needed to go to find Forest Grove Baptist Church. When we arrived services were just coming to an end at the small church and, not surprisingly, we found a few relatives standing outside the doors talking amongst themselves. After a couple brief conversations, we headed back and began walking round finding that we were related to nearly every other person, in one way or another, throughout the cemetery.

In the back right of the granite field, under a large tree, we found my great great grandparents, Roy and Sallie (Clapsaddle) Teaford. I have seen their headstones in pictures before but, as many of you know, it is a completely different experience seeing them with your own eyes. From this corner of the cemetery we slowly walked back toward the church until we found two more of my great great grandparents, Nicholas and Laura (Redcross) Love.

It was especially moving since now I have been able to visit, between all the cemeteries that I have visited, four generations of my family. My grandparents and great grandparents in Pennsylvania and now my great great grandparents and great great great grandmother today. However, what struck me most about the day was when we turned around just before leaving and I was able to see all four great great grandparents in one peaceful picture.

The following day, after our morning spelunking, we stopped by another cemetery in an attempt to find my great great grandfather's first wife. After even more dirt and gravel roads than the previous day, we were finally able to find Bethel Church tucked back into the woods on a one way road. The cemetery was just on the other side of the small creek where my dad and I walked up and down every aisle. In the end, much like Leverington Cemetery, we couldn't find her name or family anywhere among the headstones that were still visible and legible. This one is going to take some more work. Hopefully this time the church has some accurate records.

A couple of days later we visited the last cemetery of our trip while atop of Bear Mountain in Amherst County. While we were only able to find the names of a couple generations, I am certain that we were in the presence of many more generations at the Monacan Burial Ground. It took some effort, much more than the first time we visited a few cemeteries, but it was well worth the time, effort, and emotions. I am glad that we took the time to visit while in Virginia.

Putting The Pieces Together

In recent months I have made a little bit of progress on the family tree tracing back a number of lines a couple of generations and finding out a few additional details of some of my ancestors. One line that I keep coming back to lately is that of my great great grandfather, John Uttley. While I never knew much about this line growing up (and I still kick myself for not talking to my grandmother about genealogy when she was alive), there has been a lot of progress made in finding out some of the details.

Last year, through online research, reading through a variety of books, sorting through brief mentions in the local newspaper, and calling various city offices, I was able to piece together a few facts about John Uttley and his career in the Philadelphia Police Department. It wasn't much but I was able to find out that he was appointed to the police force by Mayor Stokley on May 6, 1876 and assigned badge #596. After over five decades on duty, he retired from the force in 1931 having reached the rank of Sergeant. Because the official records for the police department have long since been destroyed, this is all of the information that I could find on the career of the man who helped raise my grandmother.

The same record that provided me with his retirement year, his death certificate, also listed some very important information… the names of his parents. While I am still searching for additional information on the Uttley line, his mother's tree proved to be more fruitful. John Uttley obviously got his longevity from his mother, Charlotte Noblitt (also found as Noblit, Noblett, and Noblet), as they both died as nonagenarians. In fact, according to her obituary, she was believed to be the oldest living resident in Manayunk at the time of her death at age 93 in 1903.

NONAGENARIAN DEAD

Mrs. Charlotte Uttley, of Manayunk, Aged 93, Succumbs

Mrs. Charlotte Uttley, 93 years of age, believed to have been the oldest resident in Manayunk, died on Friday at her home, 4513 Ritchie street, and will be buried this afternoon from St. David's P. E. Church of that place. She was the oldest member of that church.

Mrs. Uttley was born in 1810 in Wilmington, Del. Her father was Thomas Nobblit, a veteran of the War of 1812. In early life she was married to Joseph Miller, who died about sixty years ago. Subsequently she married John Uttley and moved to Manayunk, where she spent fifty years of her life. She was the mother of ten children, four by her first marriage and six by the second. Her family were noted for longevity, one uncle, known as "Dell" Nobblit, having attained the remarkable age of 103 years.

While death certificates in 1903 don't provide the same valuable information as later official forms, her obituary did offer some additional leaves as her father, Thomas Noblitt, was mentioned as having served in the War of 1812. This is always great information to find so, with those new details I started looking for his pension application. Days of searching and nothing was found. Could it be that the information in the obituary was wrong?

This happens more often than people realize, when obituaries are written, especially those authored by non-family members, there are assumptions made. Maybe Thomas was older than the reporter realized. Maybe he wasn't in the War of 1812. Once I made this adjustment to my search criteria, I found the answers I was looking for. The pension application and supporting documents from the Commonwealth of Pennsylvania confirmed his service in the Revolutionary War. Charlotte was actually conceived later in life long after Thomas Noblitt's military service… longevity is obviously part of the Noblitt legacy.

Recently, I also made an interesting discovery to expand the branches out further in this line. While attempting to learn more about this line I came across a book, *Genealogical Collections Relating to the Families of Noblet*, published in 1906 by John Hyndman Noblit. The surname was close enough that I had to take a look inside these digital pages and found that this was our family. Not only does the book contain the basic information that you would find in any family tree but it also has reproductions of the actual documents from the countries where the name was once prevalent. While it doesn't have everything, it has given me a lot more information to sort through, digest, and add to this part of my family history. And, just think, this all started with a desire to learn more about a single leaf.

Lost Memorials

Over the past few years, I have visited a few cemeteries trying to find the names of family members in the vast seas of grass and stone. Sometimes I have been successful while other times it has proven to be a harder task than expected. However, during each of those visits, I remember walking by the graves of countless veterans many of whom passed away long after their service but some who were killed in action.

There were a few resting places that were well maintained and the grounds were easy to access. Others have become far from the idyllic resting place that they once were and now seem to have been forgotten. These are the places that need our attention on this day not the grills, parks, and festivities to which we have all grown accustom. In one of the more run down cemeteries that I have come across, those graves were of soldiers who died while fighting in the Civil War. It seems ironic that these resting places are the ones forgotten on this day when these graves were the original impetus for the holiday.

It makes me wonder how many parades have walked past these resting places in recent years without the participants thinking twice about those who lay, unrecognized, a few yards from their feet. I have been asked to participate in countless parades but I have never once been asked to place flags on the graves of soldiers. Maybe I should be the one who changes this lack of tradition next year.

While I enjoy the time that I am able to spend with my family, the purpose of the day seems to have been lost. The focus now seems to be on not having to go to work (different than focusing on spending time with family) and sales… the holiday itself seems to have been sold. All the while, we forget those for whom this day was meant to honor. And there is no other more visceral reminder of this change in priority than the decrepit state of many cemeteries around us especially within the city limits.

There are too many places out there that need our help not just for those for whom this day recognizes but all the families that are represented in many of these forgotten resting places. After all, you never know when you might go looking for your family and not be able to find them because their headstone has long since crumbled, sunken, or fallen to the ground. All you need to do is walk in one of these cemeteries and see the open field of grass to realize that there are countless people who will now remain nameless to realize the importance of this situation. And on this day, think about the possibility of someone buried there who gave the ultimate sacrifice who will never be recognized for their service again.

List of men transferred to the U. S. S. Tecumseh from the receiving ship North Carolina, April, 1864.

Name.	Rate.	Name.	Rate.
Allison, Saml. M.	Ordinary seaman.	Heisler, Jos.	First-class fireman.
Bartholomew, H. L.	Landsman.	Horan, Wm.	Second-class fireman.
Burns, Edw	Do.	Holland, Alfred	First-class fireman.
Berry, John	Second-class fireman.	Hurley, Jeremiah.	Seaman.
Burnett, Robt.	First-class fireman.	Hamilton, Wm.	Do.
Blagher, John	Do.	Harwood, Robt. H	Do.
Bell, John	Do.	Hatch, Chas. A	Ordinary seaman.
Brady, Wm.	Second-class fireman.	Johnson, Wm.	Second-class fireman.
Blades, James	First-class fireman.	Jay, John (colored)	Landsman.
Burns, Jacob	Do.	Kearn, Jas.	Do.
Burnes, James	Ordinary seaman.	Kane, Jas.	Second-class fireman.
Brown, John L.	Landsman.	Kindler, Jas.	Seaman.
Barry, Ambrose M.	Do.	Kostix, John	Do.
Barry, Thos. C.	Seaman.	Kennedy, Jas.	Do.
Collins, Richard.	Second-class fireman.	Lawless, Jas.	First-class fireman.
Cousins, Frank	Seaman.	Lesk, Thos	Seaman.
Cullen, James	Do.	Lyman, Gilbert A	Do.
Callahan, Pat. E	Landsman.	McAllister, Jas.	Landsman.
Cowan, Robt.	Second-class fireman.	McCue, Jas.	Coal heaver.
Churchill, Wm. J	First-class fireman.	Marts, George	Do.
Conolly, Peter	Second-class fireman.	McEllery, Michael	Do.
Christie, James	Coal heaver.	McDonald, Jas.	Seaman.
Campbell, Barney	Seaman.	Mulloy, Jas.	Ordinary seaman.
Cousins, Edward	Second-class fireman.	McGuire, Nicholas.	Landsman.
Collins, Rich. T	Ordinary seaman.	Owston, Jas. C.	Seaman.
Chapman, Geo.	First-class fireman.	O Brien, Wm.	Do.
Dalton, Jas. L.	Landsman.	Pemberton, Chas. J. (colored).	Do.
Derris, Chas. C. (colored).	Do.	Packard, Chas. A	Ordinary seaman.
Deans, Robt.	First-class fireman.	Powers, Walter	Seaman.
Davis, Thomas.	Seaman.	Parker, Peter E. (colored)	Landsman.
Dean, Chauncey P.	Do.	Rayner, Jas.	Coal heaver.
Delano, Nat. B. (colored).	Landsman.	Roberts, Wm.	Seaman.
Duval, James.	Ordinary seaman.	Smith, Jas.	Second-class fireman.
Davis, Wm.	Landsman.	Thom, Jas.	Ordinary seaman.
Evans, Chas.	Second-class fireman.	Worth, Jacob B	First-class fireman.
Foster, Fred	Ordinary seaman.	Wrenn, John	Coal heaver.
Francis, Chas.	Coal heaver.	West, Wm. C.	Do.
Finn, Jas.	First-class fireman.	Williams, John	Seaman.
Fletcher, Henry	Do.	Walker, Edw	Do.
Grady, John J	Landsman.	Williams, David	Do.
Gould, John	Seaman	Wilson, John	Landsman.
Hannible, Chas. (colored).	Landsman.		

Veteran's Day Genealogy

As it is Veteran's Day I have decided to dedicate this post to some genealogy work. While many men and women in my family have served in the armed forces over hundreds of years, there is one story that has come to the forefront this year as one of both heartbreak and sacrifice. This is the story of Jacob H. Wirth.

The original story that was handed down through the family was that Jacob H. Wirth was a licensed Baptist minister who died aboard the steamer USS *Tecumseh* when it was destroyed by a rebel torpedo in Mobile Bay, Alabama during the Civil War. This was according to records found in the minutes of The First Baptist Church of Manayunk dated 29 August 1865. While I don't know about the minister part of the story, I have been able to find substantiation of his service and of his death.

To give you a little background, here is the summary for the USS *Tecumseh* from the Naval History and Heritage Command website:

> USS *Tecumseh*, an iron-hulled, single-turret monitor, was launched 12 September 1863, at Jersey City, New Jersey. Although slated to strengthen Rear Admiral David G. Farragut's West Gulf Blockading Squadron for operations against Confederate fortifications guarding Mobile Bay, *Tecumseh* served temporarily with the James River service of the North Atlantic Blockading Squadron. To guard Union shipping against Confederate forces, the Union Army and Navy worked closely together by blocking the channel to prevent Confederate warships from coming down the upper navigable reaches of the James. *Tecumseh* was instrumental during these operations, sinking four hulks and a schooner. Although *Tecumseh* was involved in a number of notable operations along the James River,

its most famous battle would be its last--the Battle of Mobile Bay.

Tecumseh arrived off Mobile Bay on the evening of 4 August 1864. Shortly after 6 a.m. on 5 August, the 18-ship Union squadron crossed the bar at flood tide and moved into the bay with *Tecumseh* leading the van of monitors, which included USS *Manhattan,* USS *Winnebago,* and USS *Chickasaw.* The ironclads passed between the fortified headlands to starboard of the lightly-protected wooden steam frigates, taking the brunt of Confederate Fort Morgan's heavy guns. Just after 7 a.m., *Tecumseh* opened fire on the fort's batteries. Meanwhile, Confederate Admiral Franklin Buchanan's squadron, centered around the heavy ironclad ram CSS *Tennessee,* sortied to meet the attackers. When *Tecumseh* veered left to engage the Confederate ram, the Union monitor hit an underwater mine or torpedo. After a tremendous explosion, *Tecumseh* heeled over and sank rapidly with its captain and 92 crewmen. As *Tecumseh* rolled over, two shells fired from nearby Fort Morgan struck the sinking monitor.

While the above gives an accurate description of the sinking, it doesn't give the visceral feeling of the act and the reaction from those in the midst of the turmoil. For this we have to look at the accounts of the men who served on vessels alongside the *Tecumseh* such as Captain Alden, commander of the USS *Brooklyn* which was the closest ship to the *Tecumseh* as it was sunk. In his report, Captain Alden writes:

"...The starboard battery was opened on the fort [Morgan] as soon as the guns could be brought to bear. Our progress up the channel was slow, owing to our carrying, as directed, low steam, and the very deliberate movements of our ironclads, which occupied the channel close ahead of us. When we had arrived abreast of the fort, by a rapid and timely fire of grape their several batteries were almost entirely silenced. At this juncture I observed the ill-fated

Tecumseh, which was then about 300 yards ahead of us and on our starboard bow, careen violently over and sink almost instantaneously. Sunk by a torpedo! Assassination in its worst form! A glorious through terrible end for our noble friends, the intrepid pioneers of that death-strewed path! Immortal fame is theirs; peace to their names..."

Of all the accounts in the Naval records, that may be the most emotional. Other accounts are more like that of Lieutenant-Commander Jouett who was in command of the *USS Metacomet* during the battle. In his report he stated the following:

"...At 6:50 the *Tecumseh* hoisted her colors and fired a gun. Fort Morgan replied. In a short time the action became general between the fort, ironclads, *Brooklyn*, *Hartford*, and *Richmond*. At this time the rebel fleet took their stations across the channel, delivering a raking fire upon our line. At 7:35, amidst the hottest of the fire, the *Tecumseh* was blown up. I immediately sent a boat to her assistance in charge of Acting Ensign H. C. Nields, who pulled to the spot where she sank and succeeded in saving 1 acting ensign, 8 men, and pilot..."

While a few men were saved, my three times great grandfather was not. Jacob H. Wirth was 28 and serving as a fireman when he went down with the USS *Tecumseh* and he is still interred in a Naval grave at the bottom of Mobile Bay. While plans have been made at various times in the 150 years since the sinking, nothing has come to fruition regarding efforts to raise the ship. At the time of his death, Jacob left behind a wife and three young daughters the youngest of which was only a year and a half old.

But that is not the end of this particular tragedy as, back home, his wife, Mary Ann Wirth (Eppright) was tending to her daughters who had contracted what is most likely smallpox (based on the east coast epidemics of 1860-61 and 1865-73). The day after Jacob was killed in action, his middle daughter Laura (born in 1861) succumbed to her illness and passed away on August 6, 1864. Three days later, on August 9th, his youngest daughter, Mary (born in 1863), also passed away.

While she was unaware of her husband's fate at the time, Mary Ann Wirth lost her husband and two of her three children with in a matter of four days. The only surviving child was my great great grandmother, Adah Mary Wirth. This was a sorrow that Mary would have to carry for twenty years before her passing in 1885 at the age of 48.

It is on this day that we honor not just those who have survived but also those who have passed. So to all those who served this country in the armed forces I thank you for your service and sacrifice. To those who lost their lives defending this country, I thank you for giving the last full measure. To those at home who have endured separation and/or loss, I thank you for your strength. These are the men and women who serve as the foundation of our nation and they should be remembered this day and every day.

Remembering The Contradiction

While his children lay in bed fighting for their lives my three times great grandfather, Jacob H. Wirth, was aboard the *USS Tecumseh* headed toward Mobile Bay. On the night of August 4th, the *USS Tecumseh* arrived off the coast of the last major Confederate controlled port days behind schedule and with little time to prepare for the following morning. That calm evening was the last time that Jacob Wirth would have to think about his wife and children before Union admiral David Farragut ordered the attack. Farragut, tied to the flagship's mainmast rigging at this point for a better view, uttered his now-famous order, "Damn the torpedoes! Full speed ahead!"

Within the first few moments of what is now known as The Battle of Mobile Bay, having taken the lead and maneuvering to engage the ironclad *CSS Tennessee*, the *USS Tecumseh* was sent to the bottom of the bay having fallen victim to one of the many torpedoes surrounding Fort Morgan. While this horrendous turn of events may have served as a rallying cry for the men and ships around him, this was far from the reality that descended upon his family at home. In an instant his wife, Mary Ann, became a widow and his small sickly daughters lost their father.

In the following weeks, the Union naval force bombarded the three Confederate forts on the bay while Federal army troops attacked from land. By August 23rd, the last fort had surrendered, leaving Mobile Bay, the last confederate port, in the control of the United States. Many engagements during the Civil War were critical to the Union victory but it can be argued that this battle was instrumental in bringing about the end of the war as it completely stopped the flow of goods to the Confederacy and eliminated what was, at times, an admirable navy.

Of course, as the battle was fought during those two and a half weeks in August, Mary Wirth struggled at home. While she was unaware of her husband's death, she spent the duration of the battle caring for and eventually burying her two youngest daughters. Only one child survived, only one daughter, my great great grandmother, remained to comfort Mary during this time of great pain and uncertainty. 150 years ago today, far from his family and his home in Roxborough, Pennsylvania Jacob gave the ultimate sacrifice and to this day he remains at the bottom of Mobile Bay.

The Samuel Ardis Mystery

One of the first things I noticed when I initially began compiling my family tree was how many ancestors grew up not knowing either their mother or their father. One of the other examples that I have previously written about was that of Jacob Worth who remains interred with his fellow Union soldiers at the bottom of Mobile Bay having fallen victim to a Confederate torpedo while aboard the USS Tecumseh. This is a tragic tale but one which has the documents and facts by which we can determine exactly what happened. That isn't always the case which is what I faced when looking at the life and death of my great great grandfather Samuel Warner Ardis.

The day following his early demise, on Monday, September 1, 1902, the *Philadelphia Inquirer* printed a story under the sensationalized headline "DEATH USED PHILADELPHIA AS A TARGET" with one of the many bulleted subheads stating "Element of Mystery in Case of Samuel W. Ardis Dispelled by Investigation". Having been printed only a day following his death, the coroner's inquest was still pending but the details suggested that heart disease played a factor. However, some of the details remained a bit fuzzy.

To that point the investigation suggested that Samuel Ardis, who was employed as a clerk with the Reading Railway Company, was taken in by a stranger on his way home after falling ill shortly after his departure from work. Early the following morning, Sunday, the police were notified that Samuel Ardis had died suddenly at the house at some point during the night. When questioned later, my great great grandmother stated, according to the report that she was in "total ignorance of her husband's movements since Saturday".

While the autopsy later revealed, and was recorded on his death certificate, that the cause of death was pneumonia, we will never have a complete picture as to what transpired that night. The only facts that we know are that he died just over a month after his 3 month old son, Thomas J. Ardis, passed away and left his wife to care for their only remaining child, my great grandmother, Sarah Mabel Ardis, who turned three only four days after her baby brother died. In the span of just over a month, my great grandmother lost her father and her brother with her birthday falling in between. I can't imagine what must have been going through her, or my great great grandmother's, mind as all of this is happening.

We know a little but the mystery, and questions, still remain… Did he knock on a door or was he found and brought inside? Did he know the people / person who took him in? If so, how did they know one another? Did he know that he was sick? Did anyone notice at the office or was he seemingly 'fine'? Why weren't there any signs that this could happen? All these questions I want to have answers to but know that will probably never happen.

Lost Children

One of the things that many people overlook about genealogy is the fact that it is not always about making the remarkable link to some historical figure or event. Sometimes it is about making sure that people are not forgotten. This doesn't just apply to those names that may not be part of the usual family discussions, it is about the names that may not have even carried over to the next generation. I have written about many of the people that lived interesting lives, some that may have died too soon, and others whom I simply wanted to learn more about. To date, the list is rather extensive and includes the following leaves from my tree:

- Samuel Ardis
- Jacob Wirth
- John Uttley
- Charlotte Noblitt
- William Jacob McKannan
- Percy Davis Teaford
- Cecile Teaford
- John Lewis Hallman
- William Edgar Yeagle
- John Redcross

Those are just a few of the lives that I have tried to bring back to the forefront of my family history. Many of the details were already known to various family members but there have been a few that have come as a surprise (at least some of the details). These stories are fascinating to me and I will certainly be adding to that list in the near future but, for now, I wanted to take the time to share some of the names that can too easily be forgotten. Some lives are cut short while other lives never had a chance to get started.

When looking through the census records it can be a little startling to see the two numbers listed a few columns over from the mother's name. These columns stick to the factual… number of children followed by number of surviving children. The census is a form full of facts and numbers and doesn't provide any additional insights as to the discrepancy. Seeing these two, usually different, figures has become routine for many of us conducting research on our families. However, when we dig a little deeper, when we find a name, that column is no longer filled with simple numbers. Below are just a few of the names that I have been able to find…

- I knew about my great aunt Frances Reba Teaford from the time I initially became interested in the family history. A few of her siblings are still around and have shared stories about her with me and the short life that she lived. Frances was born in Eagle Rock, Virginia to Harry Gilmore Teaford and Nettie Love in 1926. She succumb to the ravages of Tuberculosis a few years after the family moved to Pennsylvania in 1943. However, I didn't find out until later about a baby brother that was born in August 1930. Unfortunately, he passed away three months later still without having been given a name.

- Samuel Ardis and Sarah Myers had three children together including twins born on April 18, 1902. Thomas died in July 1902 (a month before his father) and Edna died in March 1903 (seven months after her father).

- My great great grandmother, Susan Laura Corner, was one of nine children born to Jacob Corner and Tamise Culp. However, by the time she turned five year old, she had already lost three of her siblings including her twin sister. Calvin was born two decades before my two times great grandmother and never made it to his first birthday. Hannah was six when her baby twin sisters were born but only knew them for five years. Emma Flora, Susan's twin, was just over two years old when she passed away.

- William McKannan and Susan Corner had three children, two sons and a daughter. Their youngest son, Reuben (named after Susan's brother), was born in July of 1893. He was laid to rest in what would become the family plot in May of 1897.

- By the end of 1919, William Jacob McKannan (Reuben's brother) and Helen Fulton had four children, two boys and two girls. By the close of 1922, William was a widower caring for two sons. His two daughters, Marion (1916-1920) and Helen (1919-1922), both preceded their mother in death. Helen succumbed to a stroke on September 7, 1922.

- Over the course of a single year from 1879-1880, John Uttley lost both his first wife Sallie, who passed away in January 1880, as well as their only child Charlotte who was born in February 1879 and died three months later.

- Jacob Wirth and Mary Eppright had four children. By August of 1864, Mary was a single mother of one. Their oldest daughter,

Emma, didn't even make it to her first birthday passing away at 10 months old in October 1858. The day following her father's death aboard the USS Tecumseh at the Battle of Mobile Bay, Laura died just over a month shy of her second birthday on August 6, 1864 and Mary succumb to her illness (likely yellow fever) three days after her sister on August 9th.

Genealogy is about ensuring that the family history is passed down to future generations. Sometimes those facts and events are obvious and quite well known, other times it takes some digging to ensure that we have as complete a picture as possible. As many of you know, it is usually about the tiny details. Sometimes, even just ensuring that the name of a lost child it remembered is the greatest thing that we can accomplish. This is why I continue to try to make the connections and put the pieces together to tell the larger story but take the time to make sure that these children are part of the story and not forgotten. After all, each life is part of the family.

Not Just Another Doughboy

My great grandfather, John Lewis Hallman, was born on 29 December 1894 to a farmer father in what is now considered the Philadelphia suburbs. By the time he turned seven he was helping his father support the family without a mother in his life. Nearly a decade later, when he was 16, he was employed as a driver for the Hansell family. While he had no idea what he would face later in life, it is clear that this experience would serve as a formidable introduction to the automobile.

Now in his 20's, John was working as a machinist at the Autocar Company in Ardmore. For those of you, especially locals, unfamiliar with the manufacturer, despite innovative and commercial success of their cars, Autocar retooled their plant in 1911 to focus exclusively on producing commercial trucks. Most likely, this is when John Hallman joined the company as training and new positions with the company were readily available. The largest employer in the township, he would remain with the company throughout his working life. Of course, there was one 19 month period when he was forced to work elsewhere.

John registered for the draft in June of 1917 and proceeded to wait while the conflict intensified. In December of that year, John Hallman was enlisted as a Private in the United States Army. While in basic training, the government was looking for ways to more efficiently support the new mechanical army. This lead to General Order No. 75 and the formation of the Motor Transport Corps (MTC) out of the Quartermaster Corps on 15 August 1918. At the time of its formation, this new corps recruited from within the existing ranks skilled tradesmen who were previously working in the burgeoning automotive industry. My great grandfather was one of those men recruited to serve in the 301st MTC.

The 301st was one of three units of approximately 1,150 men each that worked in the 1,000 acre MTC reconstruction park in Verneuil, Nievre (central France). During the Great War, the reconstruction park was the end of the line for service vehicles. While at the overhaul parks, when the repair of a vehicle exceeded 30% of the initial costs, they were sent to the reconstruction park for salvage. These parks were an essential part of this new kind of warfare as was made clear by the Distinguished Service Medal being awarded to Colonel Harry A. "Bull" Hegeman who was in command of the park during the war. The park was also visited in early 1919 by Generals John J. Pershing and, later, James Harbord. The MTC was dissolved after the war in 1920.

On 18 June 1919, ten days before the signing of the Treaty of Versaille, John Hallman was discharged from the Army, returned home, and resumed his employment with Autocar where he would later work with his son-in-law (another story for another day). Later that year he married my great grandmother, Sarah Mabel Ardis, and two years later they welcomed their first child, my grandmother, Isabelle. John Hallman died on 3 January 1957 less than a year after the old Autocar plant in Ardmore was torn down.

Translation Please!

While conducting searches on different family members there is a variety of information that comes up usually requiring a lot of sorting, deciphering of handwriting, and frustration when the document that really piques my interest is in another language. More often than not I am at least able to figure things out not because I am fluent in multiple languages (I haven't even mastered one) but because I know the basic format of what I am looking at. This hasn't always been the case but after you have been doing the same kind of research for a while you generally know what information goes where largely based on where you find the name you are looking for in the document.

Early on in my research, these were pure moments of frustration that usually had me clicking on the ignore button before giving the document half of a chance to reveal itself. Now I find myself revisiting the branches on my tree and sorting through those forgotten hints so that I can again sort through them to see if anything is relevant to my family tree. I guess you could say that this is the curse of the world explorer membership on Ancestry.com.

However, this is only on instance where the language barrier can prove difficult or just flat out frustrating. While Google translate and similar programs are wonderful tools they are generally only reliable when it is strait text on a website. Add in the calligraphy element as well as the fact that most of these documents are in PDF or some other unsearchable file format and there is little that Google can do to assist. And I actually ran into this issue when researching my great grandfathers World War One unit.

When looking for information on the Motor Transportation Corps on the internet there is actually a limited amount of information that can be found as it pertains to the WWI incarnation of those units. When digging even further and specifying Unit 301, there is even less information available.

After exhausting the limited resources that populated the first few search pages, I came across a PDF document of an account from one of the locals in France... you guessed it, the document is in French. Unfortunately, I understand very little of this language anymore having forgotten nearly all that I was taught in school and Google translate refused to assist in this matter.

Thankfully it is a typed account and a common language. Older documents found in dusty books are proving to be much more difficult. However, many are in the formats of which I am familiar and have provided me with a wealth of knowledge that has been added to my ever expanding genealogical database. But, and I will leave you with this thought, it would be nice to have the ability to instantly translate the material and I encourage researchers to know at least one other language and have a network of researchers who know a variety of other languages as well. You never know when your knowledge or theirs will benefit your research.

Another Generation Of Baby Photos

Each month that passes, we do our best to take a picture of our son so that we can record his growth over time. Sometimes we manage to get the picture taken on the exact day of the month while other times we might be off by a day or two. Each time we think about the pictures that we have seen of ourselves and it is hard to believe that we are now on the other side of the lens. This time, however, I didn't look back at some of my baby pictures, I looked back much further and sorted through some of the much older family photos that I discovered over the summer.

My great grandmother, Helen Fulton, was only 30 when she passed away from a stroke but there are numerous pictures from her life both from before she married my great grandfather, William Jacob McKannan, and throughout their 10 year marriage. The first picture, which prompted this post, is from about 1893 or 1894 when she was just a baby...

A few years later, we have a photo of her as a little girl taken in about 1900 (I can actually see my niece in this photo)…

By 1910 (according to the census), my great grandparents were living next door to one another. My great grandfather was living with his uncle (along with his mother and sister) while my great great grandfather was working for the Pennsylvania Railroad while my great grandmother's family moved in with her grandmother. Some things can be written off as coincidence while other situations, like this one, seem to be fate. My great grandparents married two years later which is around the time when we can surmise that this picture was taken…

A few years later, both McKannan children were married and my great great grandmother, Susan Laura Corner, was still holding her own at home while the railroad continued keeping my great great grandfather away from his family. It was during this time, in the mid-teens (I surmise early 1914 since my grandfather was born in October 1914), when this family photo was taken with my great great grandmother in the middle surrounded by her growing family...

As I have written before, by the end of 1922 my great grandfather was left a Widower caring for his two sons having lived through the loss of his wife and two daughters over the past two years. But the photos and memories remained allowing the family to remember her, what she looked like, and the happiness that filled her brief life. You never know how life progresses or when life will come to an end but the images continue to maintain the vibrant details, from birth to death, of the family history. It is a great feeling to be adding another generation of details to our tree with every passing month.

Beyond The Camera

In the last few years of my grandmother's life, she went back and forth between wanting to pass things along to many of us (I will never forget her telling me that she wanted me to have her, and my grandfather's, High School class rings) and just wanting to get rid of things "because no one would want them". Unfortunately, what she thought no one would want were the piles of family photos piled in many of the drawers in my parent's house. In hindsight, I wish I had told her that I wanted to see them from time to time and ask her who everyone was. Definitely a missed opportunity.

Thankfully there are some photos that have survived and recently I came across a few of the older photographs that I don't remember ever seeing. While sorting through the boxes and files that have been piled in my office for the past several months, I came across a Priority Mail box that my Aunt had sent to me just prior to us moving out of our old apartment. I had put it aside with the plan of opening it once we got settled and looking through what I thought would be an album of photos from when my mom was growing up.

When I finally pulled the tab on the box I peered in and saw an expected album along with an envelope. I first pulled out the bound pages and only half of it was about what I was expecting. There were also photos from long before that time back to around the year that my grandparents met. I didn't think that this discovery could get better until I put the binder aside and opened the envelope.

In this unassuming package I found, in layers and layers, a wealth of family history in images. Sliding from one photo to the next, I was unaware of the existence of each image. Some of them were simple portraits and family photos while others told a little more about the lives of the people in those images. Knowing the basic family history beforehand only added to the story behind those moments captured.

Having done the research, I know that the following photo shows my grandfather around 1910 as a driver for a local grocery store (as was recorded in the 1910 federal census).

Additionally, looking at the following family portrait (my great grandparents, grandfather, and great uncle) I can't help but think about what is happening beyond the scope of the camera. The picture was take around 1920 and shows a family of four. At one point, in 1919 and early 1920, this was a family of six (my great aunts passed away in 1920 and 1922 respectively). By the end of 1922, this was a family of three with my great grandmother having succumb to a stroke in September of that year. It just goes to show that pictures are truly representative of a single moment in time.

Of course, this is just a couple of the photos that have been shared with me and just the stories behind the photos that I have been able to piece together. There are still a lot of images that I have yet to scan, people in those photos that I have to identify, and stories that I hope to find. It is an ongoing project that I hope never ends but I need help from the family to accomplish that... I just hope that I don't come across another situation when people don't think that anyone wants these pieces of family history. I want to do everything I can to avoid that situation and prevent that regret for not talking about the photos and asking about family history. Definitely a lot of work but well worth the effort.

Valentine's Day Genealogy

Today I thought I would do something a little different but completely appropriate given the Hallmark cards that are being handed out. One of the interesting things I frequently find myself pondering when researching the various ancestors in my family tree is about how these two, sometimes completely different, people met? Most of the time this information can only be found in the stories passed down from generation to generation.

When looking through many of the documents that my great Aunt has shared with me over the years, I came across a single page on which she has typed up what is basically a summary of her father's life. Many of the facts are easy to find in the census, birth certificate, marriage, and death records but there were also details not contained in those documents including a little about his work history as well as, and what is most appropriate given the subject of this post, what brought my great grandparents together. Here is exactly what my great aunt wrote about her parents:

Harry was the son of LeRoy and Sally Clapsaddle Teaford. He was one of nine children. He was born in 1895 and died in 1963. His first employment was as a quarry worker in a local mill that his father managed. He became interested in farming and had a love for horses. In 1916 he met Nettie Love of Sugar Tree Hollow. Nettie and her sister were accomplished equestrians. Nettie won several awards at local fairs where she rode English (side saddle) style. Their mutual interest in horses brought Harry and Nettie together and they were married in 1917 at the Eagle Rock Baptist Church. Shortly after they moved to Lorraine, Ohio. They stayed in Ohio only a short time and moved back to the Eagle Rock area. Harry began working as a farmer and over the following years worked for several large farm owners. His favorite position was with the Graham Burhnman Farm in Gala. During their time in Virginia the family had twelve children. All twelve children were born in Virginia.

However, more often than not, we don't have these stories written down for us. Many times we have to try and find and fill in the details with the documents that we do have. Such is the case with my great grandparents on my mom's side of the family. Basically, the census is what really reveals how they met and given the fact of with whom they were each living at the time, it really is a matter of what some would call fate. My great grandparents, William J. McKannan and Helen W. Fulton, can be found listed in the 1910 census living next door to one another. Both 19 at the time, Helen's family was living in her grandmother's house while William was living with his mother and sister at his uncle's house... his father, my great great grandfather, was working for the Pennsylvania Railroad in Trenton, New Jersey at the time. Two years after the census was taken William and Helen were married. Unfortunately, as I have written about before, it was a marriage that wouldn't last.

Sometimes other forces intervene in order for fate to take hold ensuring that what was meant to be becomes reality. It is true in my family tree and it is true in how my wife and I met. There are countless factors that brought us to that Barnes & Noble in Bryn Mawr that particular night when I, having just published my book "Kaddish Diary", was giving a reading and my wife was working the floor. It was that instant when we, coming from completely different backgrounds with vastly different experiences, met for the first time each of us taking the chance and getting to know one another. The same chance that my great grandparents took when they first saw one another.

Finding Family

· ·

Friday was a different kind of road trip for me and my wife as I took her to visit some of my family members whom she had never met before. In fact, I had never been there either as my family isn't one that visits cemeteries. As I had no idea of where we were going it was time to call for backup so I had my mom join us for the four hour trip that took us to Roxborough (Philadelphia), Lafayette Hill, and Conshohocken.

None of the locations were very far from our apartment but each stop was a completely different world in comparison to our previous excursions. Getting to the different places was a breeze as my mom knew exactly where to go but, after that, the specific locations of the graves had been lost in the twenty to forty years since her last visit. It made for an interesting afternoon of searching but that wasn't what held us up and took the most time.

Our first stop was to Leverington Cemetery on Ridge Avenue in Roxborough. No longer active, graves there date back to the mid 1700's and serve as a microcosm of the history of Philadelphia and, in broader terms, the evolution of our country. Unfortunately, curiosity and a sense of history were not the dominant feelings that washed over us as we entered through the old Iron Gate. Instead I was overwhelmed by shocked sadness as I guided the car along the ruts that ran down the middle and looked out the window at the broken, tipped over, and unmarked graves that litter the cemetery.

While I did come across one family marker and another potential relative (still working on the surname in our tree) we were unable to locate one of the other headstones that I know is on those grounds or any with the Wirth surname for that matter. With nearly 50% of the headstones missing, broken, sunken, tipped over, or illegible I am not surprised. As if there wasn't enough on the genealogical research list I am now going to have to see who owns / runs the cemetery (the church no longer does), find the burial records, and get in touch with both the Grand Lodge of Pennsylvania (many of the unkempt graves are those of Masons) as well as the Philadelphia Police Department to see if they are willing to mark my family's grave (John Uttley was a Philadelphia Police Officer in Roxborough (Ward 5)). I guess we will just have to see what happens.

After an exhaustive search for headstones no longer at Leverington we made our way to Barren Hill Cemetery in Lafayette Hill. Many of the family names found in Leverington can also be found in Barren Hill as, over the generations, families slowly moved further away from the city / Roxborough and into the suburbs / Lafayette Hill. Of course, there was also the fact that city cemeteries tend to become full after about 150-200 years and people need to look into alternatives.

Barren hill was a much quicker and more pleasant experience as the grounds were well maintained (just a few tilting headstones which is to be expected) and everything, at least in the section we were in, was legible. What made it exceptionally easy was that the family plot could be seen from the small, but paved, road that ran through the middle.

And on the headstone was 2 ½ generations of my mom's family from the first born in the United States in 1868 after the family came over from Ireland (along with his wife and her brother) to my great grandfather along with his two wives (his first wife died when she was 30) along with the unused plots (marked but not updated since his death in 1981) for my grandfather and his brother (unfortunately his sisters are in the family plot as they passed away when they were three and four years old). As you can see there are many different families represented and many different people listed on both sides of the headstone.

From Lafayette Hill we made our way to Gulph Christian Cemetery in Conshohocken. Here we found two generations of my dad's family. Again, this is a cemetery that is very easy to get to and our family plots are actually visible from the main road if you know where to look. Even being so close this was still my first time to the cemetery. These graves represent my family's move up from Virginia and into Pennsylvania as both my grandparents and great grandparents are buried there.

It is also the only marked veteran's grave that we came across during our afternoon travels as my great grandfather's headstone marks his participation in World War I. I specifically used the word marked because my uncle is working on getting a flag holder on my grandfather's headstone to mark his service in World War II. Graves previously found, and missing, also need to be marked in such a fashion.

In the end, it was a day of mixed emotions. I am glad that I was finally able to go visit these cemeteries for the first time but I am also left with a great sadness in the state of Leverington and in the fact that I have not previously gone out and looked for my relatives. At least now I know what needs to be done and I am motivated to do all I can to preserve my family's history and the memory of those who should still be honored even by those of us who are a part of a generation who never knew them in life.

Reminded Of Grandpop

I never got to know my grandpop. He passed away only a few years after I was born so everything that I know about him is second hand. Over the past few years I have been uncovering pieces here and there about his life. From what I have been told he was, putting it nicely, a bit of a complex man but, in the end, knowing my father and my uncle he must have done something right.

The complexities began the day he was born. As I have been told by both my great aunt and others in the family, his name was the first unique thing about him. The day that my grandpop was born my great grandfather decided that the best place for him to be was at the bar. I guess in Appalachia you have to earn the nickname "White Lightening". This did not sit well with my great grandmother so she took revenge by naming her son after a former boyfriend and the doctor who delivered the baby. That is how the name Percy Davis (first and middle names) got its start in my family.

Later in life, with no work to be found in Western Virginia, my grandpop was the one who moved the entire family to Pennsylvania. Not long after that he enlisted in the Navy during World War II and served on the USS Cole crossing the equator several times during his service. I was reminded of both of these aspects of his life as I was recording the brief life history written by my great aunt.

After the war, with his family already started, he worked with my great grandfather at the Autocar factory in Ardmore, Pennsylvania. A facility that was less than a block away from my lodge. It is that connection which prompted this post. As I was calling the long standing members of the lodge, I dialed a particular number and spoke to a brother in his early 80's. While I only knew him as a brother he recognized my last name.

At first I thought he was talking about my uncle but after he offered a few more details it was clear that he was talking about my grandpop. He remembered him from his days (decades actually) as a member of the Narberth Volunteer Fire Company. As a Captain, I guess people remember you even decades later. Heck, I have met a brother or two that remember my dad and my uncle as volunteers with the ambulance corps.

It isn't much but at least I am able to learn a little about him. And as is often the case, it only takes a few details to begin a story and that is exactly what I plan on doing. Maybe if I can add some more details and connect, in a more concise manner, all of the events in his life I might be able to get to know my grandpop a little better.

Cecile's Story

I was recently given a copy of a few pages my great aunt wrote about her life. I have talked with her many times over the past few years about genealogy, her life, and all the memories that she is happy to share with family. Now in her early 90's her memories are still there just a little harder to access and, unfortunately it has been some time since I last spoke with her. I should change that in the coming weeks especially since we can now share some more information with her about her roots for which she has always been passionate.

A recent dedication event in Elizabethtown had me thinking about all of the veterans in my family and while there are many stories that have been told and many that have yet to be recorded, my mind immediately thought of my great aunt and the pride she has in her service in the Marine Corps during World War II. She has led quite the interesting life and while the following is by no means complete, I wanted to record her words as she wrote them. While I will write a more complete story about her early years and service at a later date (as those are the most vivid memories that she described to me in her advance age), here in her own words is her "Life History":

> Grew up in Virginia. My mother was a very disciplinarian on us. I loved to be with people old (although scared of them) and young. After school at age 18 (1941) I came to Pennsylvania – had a hard time becoming a Yankee but as long as I could go home to Virginia for visit I gave in and became to like it. My first job was Freas Glass Works in Conshohocken. Mr. Freas didn't have a job for me but took me on because I had the determination to survive.
>
> The Marines were recruiting for women – I joined being first Lady Marine. I was sent to Camp Lejeune, North Carolina for training then to school for placement. My last assignment was Arlington, Virginia on the cemetery

grounds – it was a great place to be. I had the pleasure to do recruitment and cooking school taught by a Johnson & Wales Culinary School Where I had the rank of Sergeant. Where I met Truman and Bess and Margaret on several occasions. I did voluntary work at Bethesda Hospital and Walter Reed during off duty for hours. All five of us decided to take pilot lessons where I turned the stick too fast and turned the plane upside down when I landed. I never went back. It's called a drop out.

The war was over. I came home, picked up where I left off. Alan came home from the Army. We got married in 1945. Bought our first home in West Conshohocken. Alan, after some persisting, became a buyer at Chatlins [?]. I had some jobs, Lil Tire [?] and Hale Pump, but a stay at home mom. We moved to Mechanicsburg for short time where we were involved in school and church. I joined a golf club which I always had to be in some sport and chose golf. Son Alan was always in sports and Janet had Ballet and calisthenics.

Now they are grown and we are free to travel which we did. Alan always took me back to Virginia – he enjoyed it as much as I. We did genealogy as a hobby. Now my children said they never knew anything about me. I belong to the Marine Corps which was in Conshohocken home and school PTA. Conshohocken Junior Women's Club, [?], Valley Forge DAR, Women's Marine Corps Military Monument at Arlington Cemetery, Car and Auto Club Norristown, and Church Deacons, Women's Fellowship,??? and other boards.

The most rewarding thing I can do and enjoy is helping people even if a visit to the nursing home. Or where I can do a little bit at my age. The Lord has blessed me I feel with an ongoing gift and I thank him for it. As I leave this world, I can only say thanks to all the wonderful people left behind. I love y'all.

Searching For My Great Grandfather

I only had one grandparent still around when I was growing up and my grandmother and I would talk all the time. You would think that I would know the ins and outs of her family tree but the fact of the matter is that I know very little. She spoke very little about her childhood so all I really have are the pictures from her growing up to go by.

However, there is one person that is missing from every photograph which isn't much of a surprise since I never remember his name having ever been mentioned in conversation. This is why I know so little, less than almost any other person on my tree, about my great grandfather. Of course, my grandmother didn't know much about him either and never wanted to.

My grandmother was an only child raised by a single mother and her family in Roxborough. My great grandparents were only married for a few years before they got divorced (married in 1914, divorced in 1918) for reasons that I have no way of confirming (most of the stories revolve around abuse of some sort). My great grandmother never remarried (although she did have her friend and lived with him until the day he died) while my great grandfather returned to the Pottstown area, remarried, and had another daughter. With the exception of some census records and various other documents that is all I know about him.

I know when he was born and I know where he lived but I have little information beyond that… I don't even know when he died except that I know it was after 1953. I have been able to piece together the line from his second marriage. I know the wife's name, the daughter's name, and the granddaughter's name. Fortunately for me, the granddaughter either kept her maiden name or never married because I was able to find her listed in the White Pages.

At first I wasn't sure if it was the same woman that I was looking for but it was the right city and the right age so I looked for anything else to verify her identity. On a long shot I pulled up my great grandfather's old address and I was shocked to find that it was a match. This has got to be her.

At this point, the letter is in the mail. I hope to soon put a face to a name and, hopefully, good or bad learn a little more about my family. For now, I will wait and hope that my letter is well received.

A Return To Letter Writing

I used to write letters all the time, at least a letter a day, but over the years I have gotten away from that practice. However, I have been writing a lot of letters lately for both good and not so pleasant reasons. There are a number of correspondences that I have sent to management but there have also been a few that I have written for other reasons. It seems as though email and phone calls have become more of an annoyance for some so reverting back to a more traditional form of communication may provide more substantial results.

While I send a fair amount of snail mail as Secretary of my masonic lodge, which there seems to be a lot of this summer, the other pieces of mail have a much different purpose. I have taken a considerable amount of time off from doing the in depth genealogical research and now I am at a point when on line resources are not going to provide the additional information that I am looking for. There are a few things that come up here and there as archives are digitized but that still leaves me wanting more.

So, the first letter I wrote was to the Monacan Nation as it is now time to pursue membership in the tribe. Basically, there is a question as to how far back we need to provide documentation. Do we need to prove connection to those on the original rolls or do we need documentation of those individuals? It may seem like a small question but it has tremendous ramifications… one generation makes all the difference as the documents needed for that final step have gone missing from the archive in which they are stored. We will have to wait and see if this is going to be easy (as we have all the documents needed) or hard (and we need to find out where that one document is being stored).

Another piece of mail dropped off at the post office was to a woman living in Spring City, Pennsylvania. She is a descendant of my great grandfather and his second wife. While my grandmother wanted nothing to do with her father or her half-sister, it is time for the family to know more about that forgotten branch. I outlined the research and explained why I am reaching out in the letter but there is still no guarantee as to whether or not I will get a response. Frankly, I am not 100% certain that I am writing to the right person but all of the supporting information seems to make sense. After all, if I am correct, she is still living in the same house that my great grandfather lived in.

Next up will be pulling together all the information needed for the Sons of the American Revolution application. While I have all the documents needed, and then some, this is still going to be a project and a half. The work has already been done; it is simply a matter of organizing it in such a way as to hopefully speed up the approval process. It will be nice to finally have this off my plate after a year languishing on my to-do list.

So that is the plan at the moment. This, combined with whatever my aunt and uncle can find out during their upcoming trip to Virginia, will hopefully fill in a few gaps in the tree. Until then, I think I will find a few more people I can write, email, and call. And, of course, get a lot of editing done on the tree as it is looking a little ragged and is in dire need of pruning.

Car Conversation

On my way home from the office last week I decided to take a chance, pick up the phone, and follow up on a letter I had sent the previous Monday. It was sent in the hope of finding a few missing pieces on my mom's side of my family tree. After a few rings a woman picked up the phone clearly not recognizing the number. On the other end of the line was a woman who was a bit surprised by my correspondence but happy to share everything that she knew about my great grandfather, William Edgar Yeagle.

My great grandparents were married in 1914 and soon after had my grandmother. Within a few years they had divorced and not long after that, in about 1920, my great grandfather had remarried and had another daughter, Alma. The woman I spoke with was Alma's daughter who, as it turns out, was raised by her grandfather and still lives in the same house that he did many years ago. She knew her grandfather well and was raised by him when her father left. She knew that he was married once before but she was told a completely different story as to what happened in the first marriage. As it turns out, after my grandmother refused to have anything to do with him or her half-sister Alma, my grandmother's name was forgotten. Only the story remained as to what caused the marriage to dissolve.

The facts passed down in my family were rather clear cut… William was an abusive drunk disliked by my great grandmother's family. Having a child did not change that fact and, in the end, divorce was the only option. After that, my great grandmother took her child and moved in with her father. He would serve as the male figure in my grandmother's life until his death in 1941 at the age of 92.

It should be no surprise that this was not the same story that was passed down in William Yeagle's second family. The story that I was told over the phone was that William owned a bakery but was working too many hours for my great grandmother. So that he wouldn't work so much, she forced him to sell the bakery. Not long after that she left him despite his efforts. Not liked by my great grandmother's family, he was cut off from his daughter.

So, the only commonality between the stories is that my great grandmother's family didn't like him. But let's take a step back and look at the other facts that we have. While there is a William Yeagle who owned and operated a bakery during that period of time it was not the man that we are discussing in this post. It was his uncle, William Ludwig Yeagle. Furthermore, in every census record and directory listing from 1900-1952 at no point was he ever listed as a baker. Seems like that part of the second story doesn't really hold up.

What about the version of the story that was passed down in my family? Well, in those same census and directory records, interspersed between various other occupations, we can see that on several occasions William Edgar Yeagle lists his occupation as Bartender (basically he bookended the Prohibition Era with official listings as a bartender). Makes you wonder what he was really selling as a 'salesman' during that time of illegality. While that alone is not enough to verify this version of the facts, I tend to believe my family's story. Why? Because of a simple fact that my three times great grandfather was a Philadelphia Police Officer for 54 years and there was probably good reason for him not liking him.

While I look forward to meeting this woman and discussing some of the missing branches in our tree, I do so carefully knowing that many of the initial 'facts' already don't add up. Of course, this is part of the process when researching your family. Sometimes you will have two sets of information completely different from one another and investigate to see which option makes the most sense. It is all part of the process of filling in and pruning the family tree.

What's In A Name?

One of the hardest if not the hardest decision that my wife and I have had to make was when we had to come up with a name for our son. We went back and forth countless times and consulted more books and websites than I can recall each time writing down anything that appealed to us. We couldn't decide between choosing a traditional Jewish name and those names that can be found in our extensive family trees. After we each wrote a few options down we would share with one another. This eliminated many of the options. More still were eliminated when we considered the names of some of our young relatives.

After several months going back and forth we had a few options both of first names and middle names, Jewish names and family names, some that we both really liked and others that had a certain amount of indifference with one or both of us. About a week before our son arrived we sat down and looked at the options that we both liked. We played around with the names switching between first and middle as well as family and non-family names. We also considered some of the surnames on my wife's side for the middle name... after all it has worked for me.

I guess there were about 5 first and 5 middle names that it came down to. Not being able to figure out what exactly fit our son we both took turns just saying them out loud to see what sounded right. This is when we notice something very special. Each time we read the names our son decided to cast his vote. It didn't matter whose voice, he consistently kicked, punched, or head butted when we would say each name... one first and one middle. Not many parents can say that their son chose his own name but we can.

His first name is one that runs throughout both sides of my family. When looking throughout the tree I see it across many branches with various surnames in tow: Teaford, Hallman, Uttley, Redcross, Cooke, Clapsaddle, Ardis, Noblit, and a few others. It runs throughout the generations and it has always been a family name. In addition to the recent significance and honor that the name carries it was also the name of my great great grandfather Uttley, a member of the Philadelphia Police Department for over 50 years, who raised my grandmother after her parents divorced. My 5th great grandfather Redcross, member of the Monacan Nation and Revolutionary War soldier. My great grandfather Hallman who served in WWI. My 5th great grandfather Noblit, one of the early residents of Middletown Township in Delaware County who saw much of his property seized during the Revolution.

With our son selecting his first name from my side his middle name had to be one of significance in my wife's family. Thankfully our son agreed and chose a name which, according to what I have been told is the name of the last in a long line of Rabbis on my wife's side. My wife's great grandfather Greenburg may have passed nearly a decade before she was born but his legacy still lives to this day. Born in Romania and having come to the United States around the turn of the 20th century as a child, he supported his family the best he could and raised my wife's grandmother whom she still misses. In the end, our son chose names from the men who raised both of our grandmothers to which we were very close. He also made picking a Hebrew name really easy.

We did consider the origins of the names (which did seem to fit our son) but the family meaning behind them is far more significant. While we have both given the short answer during the course of conversations, now you have the full story behind the name. Our son has a part of each of us, myself and my wife, but more importantly he carries with him a long family history on both sides of which he can be proud and all he has to do to remember that is look at his own name.

Pulling Together My Own Story

Whenever the topic of family history enters the discussion we are always talking about the past… when we came over, who fought in what war, interesting occupations, etc. Anyone interested in genealogy is familiar with the cadence of these conversations and knows that it doesn't take long before a common thread is discovered between two families… although sometimes it is also interesting to discuss the differences. We, as family historians, are always digging into the past to try and find those additional details that have previously eluded us or find new information seemingly lost to the family for generations.

That seems to be the pattern and the routine with which we are intimately familiar. However, while this may be the bulk of our research, there are other areas of family history that are too often overlooked. The first is something that I have written about before which is to talk to those relatives who are still with us and learn what you can about what they know about the family as well as learning about their own life. We spend all this time trying to fill in gaps and too often the generations that are still with us are overlooked and, when they are gone, we will be back at the beginning trying to put the pieces together.

This covers the vast majority of the family history but there are still pieces that are usually left in the box. Our own lives, while not as interesting to us as the lives we have spent so many hours dissecting, are also an important part of the family tree. Since we are cognizant of the process and the details that are so important to the complete pictures of generations, we are in a position to ensure that our generation is represented. For me, part of my story is in the pages of my blog, and this book, but that is only a recent snapshot with occasional glimpses into my own past.

We have a duty to our own family and to future generations to ensure that all the stories are told, across the generations, including our own. It may seem self-centered or even egotistical and pretentious to some but this is not something that we do to brag about this or that, it is a means to keep a complete history of the family. So, the next time you sit down to explore a few more data bases, take a few minutes and write down a couple of facts about your own life and, when you get a chance, write down questions that you can send to your siblings, cousins, aunts, uncles, parents, etc. Before you know it, you will have a pretty long list to include in the annals of your own research.

Restarting Our Tradition

Years ago my wife and I would pull together a holiday newsletter recapping the previous year which was always well received by family and friends especially those that we hadn't seen in a while. This was in lieu of a card and was usually mailed sometime between Hanukkah and Christmas each year. The last time that we pulled one of these together was in December of 2012... it has been some time since we took part in this tradition and we are determined this year to once again send out a family newsletter albeit a little later than in the past.

When we decided that we were going to restart this tradition the question that we had to answer was whether we would return to the format that we used before or would we take the opportunity to pack in three years of updates into a single, long, mailer. There certainly wasn't a shortage of content from the previous twelve months and most people to whom we would be sending the newsletter read my blog on a regular basis. However, even given those two things we decided to go ahead and offer quick updates in a variety of categories encompassing the past three years but focusing primarily on this past year.

We had actually planned on getting this out last month but time has not been kind to us over the past several weeks which has left this project on the back burner. To be honest, this was primarily my fault as much of the content I pulled and condensed from my blog. My wife had already created the template and written the sections that would have simply be inappropriate for me to write so the onus was completely on me. Thankfully, we have both been able to update our address books so that part is taken care of as well.

I know that many of you are looking at this as yet another project on the inexhaustible list of items but this is an important part of our own tradition and what we want to have marking each year as a family. Plus, for me it is the summary that everyone seems to ask for understandably not wanting to sift through the hundreds of posts from the previous year. This is our opportunity to look back on, reflect, and report to those we care about what life has been like for us the previous year. And, down the road, in addition to being a simple addition to the family history files, it will be a great reminder for us all of the things that we both enjoyed and survived in 2015.

Military Ties Past and Present

Today I am not just thinking about those currently serving in the armed forces but I am also thinking about all those with whom I have crossed paths with in my life, my family members who served, and my ancestors who wore a uniform. When I stop for a moment to reflect on all of these people it is amazing to think about how extensive that list is. And that list only gets longer when I consider those I shared a barracks with in the summer of 2002 and those I only knew in passing while at Norwich prior to my time in basic training.

When I think of my family my thoughts first turn to my father, my grandfather, and my great grandfather. I know a little about each of their times in the military and the rest I have done my best to put the pieces together. My father served in the Army during Vietnam, my grandfather in the Navy during World War II, and my great grandfather served in the Army during The Great War. These are only three men without whom I wouldn't be the person I am today for a myriad of reasons.

When I look further back in the family and across the many branches, all branches of the military are represented including my uncle on my mom's side who served in the Coast Guard, my uncle and great uncle on my dad's side who served in the Air Force, and my great Aunts who enlisted in the Marine Corps during World War II. All branches represented throughout the course of history from the French-Indian Wars to the present day with several cousins still under contract with the government. It really is quite the extensive history.

While the family stories are things which come up on occasion (and there are some good ones), I hear a story or two at least once a month from many of the brothers at the lodge. These men represent over 75 years of military history from both peace time and times of war with many of them sharing vivid accounts of their service when the moment calls for their wisdom.

It really is an interesting mix of experiences that have been shared before and after meetings.

Of course, there are the men with whom I attempted to serve. Some I remember vividly while others remain nameless in my memory. I have lost track of nearly all of them with only a single connection remaining to that brief time in Missouri. I regularly wonder about what happened to many and I think about what might have been the result had I completed training along with the rest of the "House of Pain".

I am grateful to all these men and women that have served as well as those to whom I have no personal connection and I encourage you to think about the connections that you have to the various branches of the military. You may be surprised as well to find so many links to the branches that have safeguarded our country. Not everyone serves but we all benefit from the service of those who have honorably donned the uniform.

A Gift For Dad

My dad is one of those people that doesn't really talk about his Army service or his time in Vietnam. Every once in a while I would catch a little bit in conversation but it has taken time to get a relatively complete picture. Because of this, he hasn't ever really been recognized for the sacrifices he made right out of high school. With that said, I have never heard him say that he regretted going into the military. On the contrary, it proved to be a means to obtain an education and it definitely squared him away going from a C student athlete in high school to an accelerated progression through his undergraduate and graduate work.

My dad has achieved a lot in his life but is never one to talk about his accomplishments. While there isn't much that we can do about this (especially in regard to his professional career), there are some small steps that we have taken as a family in recent years to try and at least acknowledge his military service. This included having my dad at the lodge last year for Veteran's Night. Not only was it nice to have him sitting in the lodge with me but it was great seeing him recognized alongside his brother and other veterans in attendance for their service in the armed forces. It was also nice seeing him recognized at the Family Reunion over the summer as well.

However, my sister took it to the next level this year during her Thanksgiving trip down to Washington DC. While at The National Air and Space Museum she inquired as to the steps that needed to be taken to have our dad included in the Wall of Honor memorial which "recognizes those with a passion for flight." It didn't take long before I started receiving texts about our dad's service. Not having my files in front of me, I answered them the best I could remember (I should have more information in the future once my dad gives me a copy of his DD-214 for the family archives). By the time December came around, my sister had pulled together a pretty comprehensive profile to be included in the database. We all worked together to give my dad this recognition, our gift to him this holiday season.

After all, with the Army not recognizing him to the level that I would have liked to see, it is our responsibility to see that my dad is honored for his service. There are still small steps that we can take to do this and hopefully he will, once again, join me at the lodge in the coming year. However, the best thing that I can do at the moment is to keep doing what I am right now, writing and sharing the present and past family history with all those interested. Of course, I am also still trying to rack my brain as to how we can top this year's gift for dad because, at the moment, I have no idea.

Questions and Connections

Genealogy Wish List

This time of year, regardless of a person's faith, everyone puts together a wish list of what they would like to receive or see happen during the holiday season. Sometimes it is as simple as Ralphie repeatedly pleading for a Red Rider BB Gun while others are more complex or impossible to fulfill. This list, my genealogy wish list, leans more toward the latter while I hope that some will turn out to be as simple as Ralphie's request. So here it is:

1. Redcross/Beverly Marriage License: This is the last remaining piece that we need to definitively prove our genealogy back to the Monacan records. While we know where it should be and have seen the document listed in the indexes of the local courthouse, the actual marriage license has disappeared and no one knows where it is. There are some theories however but it is going to take a lot of time and significant effort to either prove or disprove them.

2. Monacan Nation Membership: We don't know if this is going to be possible without the aforementioned document but we need to at least give it a try. Maybe the index will be enough as it is still a state document but we just don't know. Everything else is in place we just need to pull all the documentation together, pay the application fee, and see how things pan out.

3. John Uttley's Service Record: While I have been able to track down when he was sworn into the Philadelphia Police Department and I have found his badge number and highest rank achieved (that was a long couple weeks of calls), there is little else that I can find regarding his service. During this research process, I found out that all the old police records were destroyed and that nothing is left but a basic database of names, badge numbers, and ranks. Maybe there is a copy somewhere… let's hope that is the case.

4. McKannan Arrival Date: The original surname was McKenna. First name was William. Arrival was during the potato famine. This shouldn't be challenging at all. This is going to take more luck (maybe luck of the Irish) than anything else as all existing leads have proven very little and, if anything, have created more possible links than verifying any. It's a long shot but I am going to keep pushing and sorting through records.

5. Percy Teaford's Service Record: While I have been able to find a good amount of information regarding my grandfather's service in the Navy during World War II, I haven't been able to get any additional information on his service in the Narberth Fire Department. This is one of those things that is just going to take time and me driving over there to see if they have any information. It would be interesting to read about this.

6. Autocar: Both my great grandfather and my grandfather worked at Autocar in Ardmore. While the factory is long gone I am curious to know if the records are still floating around (if they survived the fires just before the plants closed). I have reached out to the current incarnation of the company but have yet to hear anything. It would be nice to have an answer as to whether or not the employment records even exist.

7. Jacob Teaford's Story: The first generation to be born on this continent (before the founding of the United States). We know very little about him. We have more details about his father, the immigrant, and the generations since but he has remained a mystery for years. Heck, we can't even figure out who was the mother of his son Jacob from which I am a descendant. He is the reason why we are green dot bastards and it would be nice to fix that.

8. Nicolas Love's Parents: We have the names from his recently discovered death certificate but we no little else about them. We can't find a record of their marriage and we can't find any census records. While there are theories, like many other areas of the tree, we have yet to prove any of them no matter how probable one seems.

9. Maiden Names: This is always an issue in anyone's tree as even death certificates of siblings can differ from one to another about their mother's maiden name. This is just going to take more digging, marriage record research, and looking at census records for possible clues.

10. Revolutionary War Ancestry: There seem to be more and more connections found whenever I spend some time working on the tree. Many of them are confirmed but some connections remain tenuous at best. Even today I made the interesting discovery that my 6x great uncle was the inspiration for the movie "The Patriot". It would be nice to confirm them all and have those findings verified by the Sons of the American Revolution. Shocker, more paperwork!

11. The Yeagle Connection: I reached out to that side of the family before but the connection didn't last beyond the scope of our brief conversation over the phone. While I don't know what thoughts may have been going through her mind, it would be nice to reconnect and find out a little bit more about this line that has been largely forgotten about by my family.

12. Organization (Not Just Lists): All of these things need to be organized both physically and digitally. Right now there is a mix of physical and digital records spread across a couple of computers, ancestry.com, shelves of binders, and books tabbed for the relevant passages. Eventually, they will all be pulled together, organized in binders, and uploaded to the tree so that everyone can benefit from the work that has been put into this continuous search for answers.

Some of the records are nearly impossible to find as they are either confirmed as missing or destroyed. Some of the things on my wish list are just a matter of me finding the time to commit to the various projects. In all reality, I would be happy just to fill in a couple of these pieces of information and have everything available so that the entire family can learn and appreciate where we come from. So, let's see if I can be good this year and at least get a few of these things checked off!

Filling In The Foliage In The Family Tree

Recently I spent some time talking with the other genealogist in the family, my aunt, about the impasse that we are now facing. We have both spent the last several years working on the family tree trying to fill in the leaves, trim the branches, and follow the roots as far as they will go. We are now at a point where all of the information that can be found online has been found, catalogued, and added to our tree. We are at a point when it is going to take a considerable increase in effort in order to achieve even the smallest of results…. traveling and physically searching for documents.

While that is a huge part of the ongoing work that we need to get done there is also a completely different task which we need to accomplish. For much of the family we have the documents, the lineage, the connections from A to B, and we know of events that occurred in their lives. However, there really is no narrative that has been written on each of the generations to give us some color and fill in what was happening not only in their lives but also what was happening in the world around them. Facts can only tell you so much. The story is what makes the person, for lack of an original term, come to life.

Sometimes it's not about the events in their lives, sometimes it's about the lives that they lived. While those lives may seem unremarkable to many, they are part of what made this family and guided us along the way. What if my grandfather never moved the family up to Pennsylvania from the Appalachian Mountains in Virginia? What if Samuel Ardis lived past 28 years old? What if my great grandparents never divorced? What if each of the immigrants just decided to stay put?

Obviously, we will ever know the real answers to the hypothetical questions. We will also never know if the stories we tell are completely accurate. But we can at least attempt to breathe life back into our ancestors and try to better understand the lives that they lived, the hardships they faced, and the decisions that they were forced to make. This should be interesting.

A Sea Of Irishmen

⚜ ⚜

While research on my dad's side of the family has been a project shared by many family members (both close and distant relatives) over the years, research on my mom's side of the family has always been a more challenging endeavor. Where I have been able to build upon the foundation built by others on my dad's side, the land had yet to be graded on my mom's side until a few years ago when a few of us decided to break ground. It has been a bit of a slog at times but there is a lot of information now contained in our tree, a lot of family stories that have been confirmed, and a lot of documents that have been consolidated.

However, when following the paternal line on my mom's side, there is quite the thick fog when delving into the 19th century. While I have been able to have a relatively complete record of my great great grandfather's life, his father remains a mystery. Unfortunately, trying to find a specific William McKenna among the waves of Irishmen during the Potato Famine is a task that is difficult to say the least. And while the name isn't as common in Pennsylvania in the second half of the 19th century as one would think it is still nearly impossible to verify the connection in the scarce documents that I do come across.

The other consideration is the simple fact that with limited job opportunities and significant backlash against the influx of Irish immigrants during that time, there are countless countrymen that remain without official records (an informational famine)… even the census has its limitations. In fact, much of the information I have been able to find about this particular generation comes from his children and what they later reported to the census taker and wrote on various documents. In the end, we have what we are left with is a name, approximate year of birth (1840), country of origin, and approximate immigration between 1845 and 1865 (port unknown).

That leaves a rather large pool of potential candidates when trying to sift through immigration, census, limited death records, and family trees. I have a mountain of names and documents that all seem to fit in one way or another but, when I try to put the pieces together, the shape is all wrong. While this is by no means an impossible endeavor, it is one that will take a considerable amount of time, more information, and a few lucky breaks in order for us to find this generation during my lifetime. And, unfortunately, I know I am not the only one who faces this challenge.

Finding The Kelly Green Leaves

There are certain days during the year when everyone seems to assume the same nationality for one reason or another. Some people do it because they like the color green, some because they use it as an excuse to drink, and others because they just enjoy the atmosphere of the day. However, for many of us it is an excuse to look deeper into our roots. St. Patrick's Day is probably the best example of this community participation.

Being Irish was not really something that was a focus for me growing up. In fact, nationality was never really something that was a focus for anyone in my family. We were all born in the United States, our parents were, our grandparents, and our great grandparents so the tether to the boat was quite long. It wasn't until we really started taking a closer look in recent years (at least for me) that I became more interested and connected to the various heritages that I carry with me.

It started on my dad's side as I still remember driving down to Virginia in the summer of 1987 and spending the long weekend at the family reunion. This was a little different than the typical reunion that comes to mind as each person in attendance could trace back to the original German/French ancestor that arrived in Philadelphia on 27 October 1764. Good luck trying to figure out how you're related to each person.

We never knew much about all the other branches on my dad's side but that has developed substantially over the past decade or so. There is far more than just German blood in that tree as there are lines across various parts of Europe as well as deep native roots her in the United States. However, while there is an assortment of nationalities, there is only a faint touch of Irish blood on that side.

Much of my Irish heritage comes from my mom's side of the family and, growing up, we were never certain that some of our leaves were a vibrant Kelly green. Once we put a few pieces together and determined that the original surname was McKenna there was little doubt that the family's arrival in the middle of the 19th century was from Northern Ireland. Tracing your Irish roots back to the potato famine isn't very unique but at least now we know.

Like my dad's side, my mom's side of the family is also an interesting mix coming from various parts of Europe. And just like the German blood is thick on one side, the Irish blood is thick on the other. Actually, given the tendencies of each, it might be pretty watered down. So have a drink… you may find out one day that you're Irish. Sláinte!

Missing Documents

Over the past few months there have been moments when I have made surprising progress researching my family trees and there have also been instances when I have hit some pretty significant walls. No matter how hard I have tried to hit the brick or how heavy the hammer, the structure remains solid. While there is still some small glint of hope that these records will turn up, it is not an endeavor that will likely produce significant results anytime soon… I guess I will have to get the chisel out and try to find the answers that way.

After all, that is how I found the few details that we know about John Uttley's service in the Philadelphia Police Department. After dozens of calls and many hours leveraging various resources I was able to find out that while the full personnel files have long since been destroyed, there are pieces (i.e. rank, badge number, date of swearing in, accounts in the newspaper) scattered across multiple sources. It isn't much but it is a heck of a lot more than we have had in the past. Other endeavors haven't even produced this level of information.

My great grandparents (William Edgar Yeagle and Bessie Wirth Uttley) divorce is something that is still interpreted different ways depending on with whom you speak. His first family, which is my line, sees the dissolution of marriage in one way namely that it was his drinking and abuse that caused the divorce. However, his second family, according to his granddaughter with whom I briefly spoke a couple of years ago, sees things a little differently in that it was my great grandmother that caused the issues in the marriage. When I called the court records office in Philadelphia City Hall (where they got divorced), there was little information that they could share as the records have long since faded and the only information on hand was that of the actual decree (without mention of cause). But at least that record can be produced unlike some others.

The marriage certificate of Paulus Redcross and Frances Beverly continues to be one record that we are continuing to search for through various offices, depositories, and any other means available. It is something that we know exists as it is recorded in the Amherst County, Virginia ledger but the actual document seems to have disappeared. Not faded or destroyed (as far as we know) it is just gone. No one has been able to provide any definitive explanation although there are plenty of theories out there which is a completely separate topic altogether.

All of these documents have the potential to provide my family with a wealth of information (and answers) beyond what the existing documents ever could but there is significant doubt as to whether we will ever be able to read them. While we will continue seeking answers to other questions and look to fill in the family tree, these are things that we will always be looking for even if the possibility of finding them is slim. While these situations may be a deterrent for some, it only serves to motivate me to find and write the story without them (or at least try).

More Dead Ends

While I have been able to make some progress recently on tracing back along the branches of the family tree, I have also encountered a number of roadblocks. It hasn't been a matter of being able to find the right person to call, it is largely a matter of records no longer existing. Of course, there are also a few instances where I simply don't have the access to the records. Really it is the combination of these two situations that has forced me to find other avenues to find the information for which I am searching.

I previously wrote about my numerous interactions with the Philadelphia Police Department and the discovery that most personnel files have long since been destroyed. While I was able to piece together a few aspects of John Uttley's service, there are still many holes and questions that remain. However, sometimes we have to be satisfied with what we have and take some measure of contentment knowing that we have been able to confirm that he did serve, how long, badge number, and rank. Some people don't even have that much information.

I ran into a similar situation as this when I called the Narberth Fire Department to try and get more information about my grandfather who was a Captain with the volunteer company. As it turns out, after years of renovations, moves, leaks, and other instances, most of the records prior to 1970 have been lost. However, I was still able to find out that, late in life, he was on over two dozen calls. Thankfully, there are also some photos in the family from this time.

As I waited for Narberth to return my call, I also reached out to the current incarnation of Autocar now located in Indiana to see if they had any of the personnel files from the early days on the Philadelphia Main Line… this is where my great grandfather spend nearly his entire working life. I can't say I was surprised when the woman on the phone informed me that only the name has been transferred over the years and the whereabouts of the files are unknown. There still is a chance that these records exist but now it is a completely different task trying to figure out where they ended up… I guess it is time to reach out to a variety of historical societies.

Lastly, while conducting the aforementioned outreach, I also looked into trying to secure my grandfather and great grandfather's service records from WWII and WWI respectively. While these records exist, at least most of them, only next of kin are allowed to order the files. The simple translation is that I have to have my father submit the request in order to get these copies. Sometimes these extra steps seem to add up but at least there is a "simple" solution.

What I have found throughout the process and the point that has been driven home again and again is the simple fact that we, as a family, must keep our own records. If you want to know the story of your family and you want future generations to know about the family we can't rely solely on the depositories found in other places. At the same time, make it known that you have certain records and share them with anyone who is interested in learning about the generations that preceded them. In other words, don't let someone else control your family story… don't be afraid to be the family historian.

Putting Names To Faces

When my wife and I were figuring out our schedule we knew that we wanted to get together with my parents before they left for a little warm weather vacation. Fortunately, despite some other changes to our plans, everything worked out and we spent an afternoon together. More importantly, our son spent some time with his grandparents.

It was supposed to be one of our usual get-togethers over lunch and then back at the house to catch up on things (even though I talk with them every few days). It is a nice relaxing time. However, I decided to change things up a bit when, because the thought popped into my head, I decided to pull out the photo album sent to me over a year ago at this point and flip through the pages with my mom. We did a quick scan before lunch noting some of the relatives I knew, many that I didn't, and, oddly, some that I recognized but my mom didn't.

This was a long overdue project and after lunch, toward the middle of the afternoon, we revisited the photos but this time we took a closer look and I had post it notes in hand to record the names. After flipping through a few of the pages and not being able to put a name to a face on a few occasions, we peeled back the plastic and carefully pulled up the pictures from the paper in the hope that there might be some information on the back. While this didn't always work, there were a few times when it did and it allowed us to put a few more pieces together.

What we couldn't figure out immediately was the handwriting on the backs of the photos until one of the last pictures had the simple words inscribed on it "My Mother" which means that my grandfather labeled many of the photos that we had been looking at over 30 years ago. It was one of those things that we didn't expect but glad that we figured out. What was also nice was the fact that I have done so much on the family tree because there were a few times when only first names were known or 'that was her or his daughter." By having much of the tree completed, I can write down the bits of information now and put the pieces together later.

Hopefully, this is the first of many times when I can sit down with my mom and put faces to names. There are a number of other loose photos and albums stored in drawers at their house and I am eager to flip through them and finally pull together a visual history of the family in addition to the information that we already have. Who knows, maybe I can even discover something new. But, for now, it is back to the current album where I can now write (with an archival pen of course) on the backs of the photos the names of the faces on the front.

Familiar Faces

* *

When my mom and I were looking through some of the family photos there were a number of times when we could easily see some other family members in the faces of the ancestors who have long since left us. And it was interesting as to when it would hit us as there was really no guarantee whether the person's name or the current counterpart would be thought of first. At the same time, there wasn't any certainty as to which one of us would make the connection either.

In some instances my mom would tell me who someone was in the photo and then follow up with something along the lines of "I didn't realize how much your cousin looks like her." There were other times when I would see either an aunt, uncle, or cousin in one of the people and as soon as my mom told me who they were it made complete sense. And, of course, there were various combinations of this throughout our time with the album on the table in front of us.

While it is certainly clear to those who know my family, I get much of my looks from my father's side of the family. However, in looking through the photos with my mom I could see a little piece of myself in some of the pictures. I noticed a couple of little things like my hair line and posture but what really stood out to me, which I knew of before, was the handwriting that was on the backs of many of the photos. While my looks may be predominantly from my dad's side, my handwriting is, without question, from my mom's side.

Sometimes these ties are really what make looking through old photos in particular so interesting. On the surface you are putting faces to names but on a completely different level you are finding yourself and many of your other family members in little pieces of the past. It just goes to show that your family, your whole tree, plays a big role in who you are regardless of what you might think. This, of course, is in addition to the obvious genetic traits that we carry. Sometimes it is in the simple things like looks but sometimes it can be in other ways like handwriting, the way you hold yourself, and your demeanor.

For better or worse, I kind of have a mix of all those things. There are little pieces from both sides that I carry with me every day. And I am certain that there are many other similarities that I have yet to discover with some of my ancestors. So you can look at genealogy as pulling together the family history or you can look at it as finding pieces of yourself. For me, it is definitely a little of both.

A Good Place To Sleep

* *

When we first moved into our old apartment in 2011 we didn't have much to fill the space and it took some time before we were able to make the small confines comfortable. Over time we accumulated a fair amount of stuff and by the time we finally got out of that building we were able to fill much of our next townhouse rental. In fact, it was nice spreading things out across multiple rooms.

Since we first hauled everything through the door into that second rental it, once again, turned into a slow accumulation of stuff. The vast majority of the new items were not optional as we had a long list of things that our son was going to need both when he arrived and soon after. It is safe to say that this filled the rest of the rooms and overall space that we gained when we moved.

However, of all the things that we have accumulated there are a couple of items that are particularly meaningful to us. As has been made evident, family is very important to me and my wife. This is why we were excited when my mom thoroughly cleaned the family bassinet (to help with my wife's allergies) so that we could use it in our home. My grandparents bought the bassinet 75 years ago and it has been passed around the family ever since providing a bed to countless relatives.

It wasn't until after our son arrived that we were given something from my wife's side of the family with the same kind of history behind it. My wife's cousin approached us and said that she had something very special for our son. As it turns out my wife's great grandmother had knitted a blanket over 40 years ago for her cousin but, for one reason or another, it was never used. It was put away in a closet for over four decades before they decided to give it to our son.

The two came together... two families made into one. Generally, we don't have many items that carry so much history but it was nice to have just a few that we were able to use and, more importantly, that our son was able to use. For the first few months of his life our son took his naps surrounded by both sides of his family and over 100 years of combined history.

Telling Time

✱ ✱

Having spent the last couple of months sorting through family photos it was time to change things up a bit. Sometimes it can get a little repetitive looking at the two dimensional as it can be difficult at times to peer over to the other side of the lens. It is times like these when I like to pull open my dresser drawer and hold the items that have been passed down to me through the family. While there are a variety of items from rings and cuff links to spoons and other knickknacks, there is a small collection of watches that I seem to go back to more often than the other items.

The Timex at the top of the photo is by no means a valuable wrist watch. It is a very simple, heavily worn watch that my grandpop used to wear. That is where the value is for me. I don't have many memories of my grandpop but there is something about holding an item that he wore every day that brings a sense of connection and makes me wonder what that watch had been through and where it may have been as well.

The pocket watch at the bottom of the picture is something that represents both sides of my family. My great grandmother gave this Howard watch from the 1920's to my dad years ago. He added the chain where you can see his initials. A few years ago he passed this watch down to me and I have taken it all over the world while it has also served as inspiration for numerous creative endeavors in the past. It is something that represents my mom's family and, while I don't recall him ever using it, something that reminds me of my dad.

The three watches in the middle came to me at different times in my life. The Citizen on the right is the first watch that I bought and it served me well for a couple of years. The Invicta in the middle was given to me by my brother at the rehearsal dinner the day before his wedding when I served as one of his groomsmen. And the watch on the left is the one that I have worn nearly every day for the past eight years. My parents gave the Hamilton Khaki Automatic to me and it has not only served me well over the years in a practical sense but it also reminds me of my parents and their generosity whenever I slow down and take a moment to appreciate it.

All of these watches have stories behind them. Some old, some new. Some tell a little bit of the story of my family while others are simply a part of my story. However, I hope to pass these down to my son, along with the stories that I know, many years from now once I have had a little more time to enjoy them. Again, that is the true value in these timepieces.

Sifting Through The Forgotten Cards

There are a few boxes on my office bookcase that I rarely look in. They are usually tucked below the boxes that receive more regular perusals which contain the loosely sorted family photos that I have accumulated over the years and the one with the random office supplies that always seem to come in handy every now and again. These other boxes are frequently added to when certain items are deposited into the mail box but that is the most interaction I have with the box… stuffing some of the cards and invitations under the lid to be seldom seen again.

However, while continuing my organizational endeavor, I opened these boxes just to see what I had put in them over the years. It is actually a great way to reminisce about some of the past family events, recall fond memories with friends, and look back on some of the holidays that have passed. It is interesting to look at the different kinds of cards that people have given me over the years. Some serious, some touching, and others funny. It is a pretty wide variety.

There are items within these boxes that made me pause for a minute and think about all that has changed over the years. All these cards and invitations are things that have already happened and with so much to look forward to in the future, it is a unique dichotomy when you hold these items in your hand. And, of course, there are some items, some cards that have taken on an entirely new meaning as I have gotten older like seeing my grandmom's signature on a holiday card. I still miss getting those cards every year.

There are also the items that I am glad that I have held onto rather than simply pitching shortly after receiving them. I guess it is part pack rat and also part knowing what has become important to me when putting together the family history. Some of these types of things, the simple cards and notes, are more often than not lost during the course of life. These things are really what bring the memories back, sometimes more so than pictures. Being able to hold these items and see the handwriting of my grandmom, my parents, and my wife are what can trigger the memories of great times in my life. I should really open this box more often.

Rediscovering What Was Already Discovered

My wife and I decided to dedicate this weekend to cleaning and our son finally let us get the much needed work done around the house. With the washing machine humming, sloshing, and twirling in the background, we went from room to room cleaning, organizing, sorting, and packing. It took the entire weekend to get most of the house done and by the time my wife went to bed on Sunday night the only two rooms remaining were our offices. This is a wholly different task altogether as we both have more paperwork than storage space and more books than shelves. It is going to be interesting but hugely satisfying when it is done.

With my wife and son asleep, I ventured down into the basement and began sifting through the rows upon rows of shelves. I went down there with the goal of filling one box of books that had little value to me at this moment. As someone who enjoys information and having resources readily available, this is not a very easy process… many of the books that I have collected over the years are those that contain information that has yet to be digitized. Contrary to what some people say, not everything can be found on the internet. After about 30 minutes, I actually was able to fill a box and clear a shelf for the binders of new research that was going to be added. It came down to a small sampling of books that I know I can find again when I have the space.

Once this part was done, I began flipping through the binders on the shelves and files stored in boxes. It really is amazing what you can find when you sit down and sift through the boxes in your office… this is especially true when it comes to genealogy. While slowly flipping through the pages and pages of notes and photocopies, I rediscovered small details that I had written on a pieces of paper while pouring through volumes and volumes of material. They are the small details (like the fact that my great grandparents were brought together by their love of horses) that I had forgotten almost as quickly as I was able to record them.

It is the dilemma of disorganization. While many of the documents and facts have been sorted and organized for later, many of these details seem to get lost in the pages. At the same time, rediscovering these details was just as interesting as when I first read them. It was nice to feel that same way about finding 'new' information and it makes me wonder what other documents I have buried (most likely from a scanning / photocopying marathon). With the rest of the house in order, I am glad that I am now in a position to take on this task... at least until the files get moved again.

Moving Our Archives

As we are slowly getting settled into our new house, all the boxes that I spent packing long into the night are starting to get cut open and the contents roughly organized. Not only are we having to put clothes away, line the books neatly on the shelves, organize the boxes of toys, and get the kitchen put together, we are also having to figure out a system for storing as well as a place to put all of our binders and boxes of photos. Of course, now that we have a home and we are not anticipating any further moves, we are taking things a bit slower this time around and really figuring out a system that works for each of us.

Thankfully, we have enough room in our house that we each have an office to go along with an abundance of storage options. However, with options and wanting to take things slowly this time around, we are falling a bit behind in getting things to a place where we can readily pull out images or information. And with things previously so scattered it was a bit overwhelming when we realized just how much we have... we knew we had a lot but we didn't fully grasp the sheer volume of research and images that we have collected over the past several years.

With a few more storage options, and more boxes, my wife has figured out her own system. While I have a few less places where I can hide the disarray, I have figured out a way to get organized and have started putting thing in an order that will allow me to pull out information I want fairly easily. Of course, this is only half of it as much of my information is still in a digital format. While there are certain advantages to this I still prefer to have hard copies and many times find it easier to pull up information rather than rummaging through files on my computer.

While there have been many attempts in the past to get all the family information and history organized, we are finally in a place when we can get it done and not worry about what would happen if we had to pack it all up and move it into a completely different space. So, for now, we are going to take a quick break from researching and focus on the archiving of our legacies. In the end, this can be just as important as finding that next new piece of information.

Who Needs A Mirror?

Can you feel the pain of a previous generation? Do your ancestors speak to you? Sometimes I run across something that, in the past, would not have bothered me but now, with my new found genealogical knowledge, causes me to stop and think. One of our trips in particular had one of those moments."

"HELP WANTED // NO IRISH NEED APPLY"

This sign really hit me and it nearly stopped me in my tracks when I saw it at the Old Jail Museum in Jim Thorpe, Pennsylvania. It played on both my heritage and my employment situation at the time as I was experiencing a great deal of flux in my employment situation and was working an hourly job at night to pay the bills (or at least some of them) while I tried to secure a salaried position in my chosen profession of public relations.

Thousands upon thousands of Irish flooded into the United States during the time of great famine in Ireland during the 1840's and 1850's. Many were greeted with the sign above and were forced north to the anthracite mines. They worked grueling hourly jobs to do what they could to support their families.

This sign both helped me to bond with the men in my family who fled Ireland, were met by those same signs in Philadelphia, and were forced to work in those same mines. At the same time, it made me appreciate all that I have... my situation was nothing compared to what my ancestors had to deal with. This sign should be motivation to anyone to keep pushing forward; this was my motivation that I would find the right position, we would find the right home, and we would find the right balance. If you let the sign tell the story you will find yourself in the sign.

Reunion Memories

I'm Still A Green Dot Bastard

* *

I have been working on the family history off and on for a few years now and I am glad every day that I started on this project. With that in mind, there are some days/weeks/months that I want to pull my hair out and I have had to take breaks here and there on the research side but, overall, it has been satisfying to see the colors being filled in on many of the leaves.

When it comes to genealogy, everyone has gaps and mysteries in their family tree and mine is no different. They are the most frustrating and rewarding aspects of this kind of personal research. You can spend days trying to answer one question and not find a darn thing. However, when you find that missing piece of the puzzle buried deep in the pages of a book or in the far corner of a database it is an amazing experience.

Sometimes you just have to collect all the records, all the facts, lay them out in front of you and figure out how everything works together. This was the case when I had to put my mind to work and figure out where the third generation came from in my family. Who was Jacob Teaford's (III) mother?

My earliest memories of learning about my family history go back to the Teaford family reunion in 1987. This is not your usual family reunion as this encompasses all branches of the tree. Anyone who can trace back to the original ancestor that came to the colonies on 27 October 1764 is welcome. Each of the six branches was assigned a colored dot on their name tag which also contained the numbered lineage below their name… I was a green dot with a question mark making us all green dot bastards.

With greater access to records in the digital age (most notably through ancestry.com) I have been pulling bits and pieces together to add to the hard copies of other, more obscure documents, which sit in a binder on my shelf. Combined with the work of previous generations and the smaller items I have been able to find I finally came up with a plausible scenario…

I think I figured out the mystery. Based on the evidence, most notably minor sections in court documents, it seems likely that Jacob number three was born out of wedlock and cared for by his father and grandparents. So, we're still bastards but at least I am comfortable in eliminating the question mark.

Of course, this was only the first of many questions that are throughout my tree and, sometimes, I wish I was still working on the first. There are many gaps in the digitization of records and I am nearing the end of the line when it comes to the information that is available online. I guess it's time to put some miles on the car and get some dust on my hands.

Preparing For The Drive...

* *

While we have no idea where the time has gone, we are now finding ourselves scrambling to get everything together for our family vacation. The last time that we took such a long vacation was nearly three years ago so there are a lot of things that have changed since then. Things are completely different now that we have our son as in the past packing for vacation was never a real issue. Looking at the piles of stuff that needs to be packed, it is amazing to think that we will be able to fit it all in the car. I don't think we have packed this much stuff since we left for Israel.

For the first time since I started with my current company, I am taking an extended period of time off away from work. Even when our son was born, I was out of the office but still working remotely. With the exception of a few phone calls and emails that I am most certainly going to have to take, I am staying far away from the world of work. It's not like I am going to have the time to take care of things as our schedule is pretty full. Here are just a few of the things that we are going to be doing and places we are going to visit while in Virginia:

- Family Reunion
- Natural Bridge
- Caverns at Natural Bridge
- Eagle Rock
- Fincastle
- Various Family Cemeteries
- Roanoke
- Dixie Caverns
- Bear Mountain
- Monacan Museum
- Lynchburg
- Lexington

- Colonial Williamsburg
- Richmond

This is a trip that I have been looking forward to for years. This is the first reunion that I have been able to attend since 1987 and I have learned a lot about the family since that time. It is a trip 28 and 250 years in the making and I am excited to see everything again with new eyes and also to introduce my wife and my son to where our family comes from.

Obviously, this is just the short list but not a bad schedule for the week. This is what we plan on doing and seeing… that could easily change and we may see more or less depending on how the week progresses. While we may have a good schedule for the extended vacation, I really don't want to stick to a hard schedule. This is a time for us to relax and spend time with family.

Our Family Was Here

I can't say I have ever been one for big Independence Day celebrations. I have watched the fireworks from a variety of vantage points from the comfort of the living room on the television screen, in Philadelphia, at the New Jersey shore, at my Aunt and Uncle's house, and while lying on the grass in my BDUs in central Missouri. However, while the temporary bright lights in the sky were never something that really interested me a lot, the day has always had tremendous meaning. While I didn't quite understand it early in life, there was still always something a little different about the day.

Of course, now I have a much more complete understanding of what makes this day such a big part of who I am. And I am not talking about the reasons that this day is important to us all, I am talking about the connection that I have, that my family has, to this day and what generations have done since to defend this country. And with those thoughts fresh in my mind, it was particularly special to celebrate this holiday with family, with the whole family, as we gathered together in Virginia.

And when I say the whole family I really mean it. This is a little different than what usually comes to mind when someone mentions a family reunion. This is not simply the immediate members that you see here and there, this particular reunion brings together all those who can trace back their genealogy to our original immigrant ancestor, Jacob Duffordt, who arrived at the Port of Philadelphia aboard the Hero on the 27th of October 1764. There are thousands in our tree with a small sampling making the trip this year to the mountains of Virginia.

As you can tell by the date, we were here before the revolution and beginning with the simple act of Jacob Duffordt selling supplies to the Continental Army, we have taken an active role in supporting and defending this country. From Jacob Duffordt during the Revolution, to his grandson during the War of 1812, countless relatives during the Civil War, my grandfather and his siblings during World War II, my father in Vietnam, and others in the family who have served more recently. All have given of themselves to ensure that this holiday remains as a day to be celebrated.

Celebrating this day with family, with multiple generations, in a place near where we originally settled is what this holiday is about for me. This was about as close to a perfect representation of the holiday that I can recall and one that I hope to relive many times over in the future. This is our holiday, part of our history, and a reminder of all the generations that came before us and the ones that still lay ahead. We have to remember our history and continue to pass on what we have learned and the experiences we have had so that future generations can look back on this day and experience the same connection.

Our Towns

❀ ❀

With the reunion having concluded the previous day, we filled the following day with a variety of stops and places that I wanted to see during our extended vacation in Virginia. Much of our morning consisted of a few trips to some local cemeteries but this essay is not about those explorations, it is about where our family lived both in the early part of the 20th and latter part of the 19th centuries.

Before moving up to Pennsylvania, my grandfather was born and raised in Eagle Rock, Virginia. This is where all of my great aunts and uncles were born as well. I guess you could say that it all started at the Eagle Rock Baptist Church where my great grandparents, Harry Teaford and Nettie Love, were married in 1917. For the first time, I was able to see the church thanks to my great uncle serving as our tour guide for the day.

Of course, before we received this guidance, we were left on our own to explore the small town. While it is clear that it was once a nice little mountain community, the town seems to have never recovered from the depression that drove my family north. While the train station still looked like it was in good working order...the car dealership had clearly been lacking that new leather smell for some time.

This is obviously not a touristy type stop but it is where we come from, it is the first time that I have been able to walk the streets, and probably the first time that my father had been there in about 50 years. While pictures and documents make up much of my genealogical research, places are also an important part of the process. Walking the same streets and seeing the surrounding mountains gave me a much better understanding of the generations of my family that called this small town home.

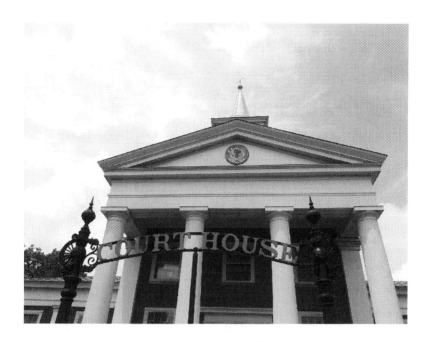

Later in our explorations we met up with a cousin in Fincastle (my aunt and uncle also joined us). Surprisingly, we were the only ones that took her up on her offer at the reunion for a tour of the capital of Botetourt County. Many of our family documents can be found in the Botetourt County Courthouse so I was looking forward to finding out a little more about the town itself. We all convened at the local museum and proceeded to walk the town as the humidity continued to rise.

Just in front of the museum was the county courthouse which served as the gateway to the west when this now modest county extended far beyond its current boundaries and deep into the Midwest. It is because of this distinction that the courthouse is recognized for its place in the Lewis & Clark Expedition. From the courthouse we walked up and down the main and back streets of Fincastle passing numerous historic sites, old houses, and quite a few churches including the one in the following photo which dates back to before the Revolutionary War.

The town tour ended where it began and our generous host concluded the afternoon with a walk through the museum. Of course, the path around the building lead us directly to the research room where we couldn't help but pour through a few of the volumes stacked on the shelves. While we didn't uncover much, it was nice to be back in the stacks sifting through all of the names. And, obviously, it was once again nice to have my feet on the same soil and stones that were once walked by many in my family decades ago.

Revisiting The Bridge

There are only a few things that I remember from the reunion back in 1987. Obviously, I remember a few of the faces and the fun at the gathering itself but one of the other things that has always remained in my mind was seeing the Natural Bridge. It is because of this memory that I wanted to return to the natural wonder now that I am quite a bit older and am able to appreciate the experience.

Of course, memories can be rather selective and while I retained an image in my mind there was little else about the brief time we spent there nearly three decades ago. Maybe it is because of this that I forgot all about the stairs leading down into the valley and the massive trees that lined the path. Once we got to the bottom and slowly made our way down the path the first sight did not disappoint and after a few family photos and listening to a brief history about the formation and ownership of the sight we proceeded down the walkway for a closer look.

From beneath the mammoth formation it was hard to believe the different roles that the bridge has played in history not just as a tourist destination (one of the first in the United States) but also as a functional formation for the production of cannon balls during the War of 1812 (molten lead was dropped from the top which naturally formed into a ball on the way down and immediately cooled and hardened upon hitting the water below). Looking back you can see the deeper water where the ammunition collected. Having reached the other side I noticed that while the other side the structure doesn't have nearly the same visual impact it still possesses an impressive presence.

Walking further along the path there is another part of the experience that is of great personal interest to me, the Monacan Living History Exhibit. It is an unassuming presentation as you approach the site with the fence hiding much of what is behind the walls but once you walk through the entry the details are impressive. The recreated (albeit downsized) exhibit offered a unique glimpse into what Monacan villages looked like during the time of first contact by European settlers (note that the Monacans are included on John Smith's map of Virginia in 1612). Some of the structures on display included spaces that would have been used for meetings, cooking and weaving, as well as shelters where people would have slept.

The overall 'village' was something to behold and the experience was only enhanced when I was able to speak at length with one of the tour guides who also happened to be a member of the Monacan Indian Nation.

From the village we continued down the path toward the waterfall. Along the way we came across the saltpeter mine which was also used during the War of 1812. This was a full service site at the time for the needs of artillery units. It wasn't long after that when we reached the waterfall. Of all the ones that we have seen in our travels it wasn't the most impressive but when thinking about what it helped to form it was well worth the additional walking.

Having walked to the end of the trail it was time to turn around and head back to the bridge. The weather was a bit questionable throughout the day both with heat and rain possible. However, the sky remained relatively clear and offered us a reminder as we approached and walked back under the bridge.

While there are many more memories that I will carry with me from this trip compared to the brief glimpses from years ago, I couldn't help but take one last picture as we approached the stairs. Oddly enough, the impression is just as strong with the last glimpse as it was with the first. Hopefully, it won't take so long this time around to return.

Sometimes You Can Feel A Place

The winding roads through the mountains and into Amherst County gave me the time to reflect on both all that we had seen up to that point and also prepare for our next experience at the Monacan Indian Museum. As a precaution, I had called the museum during our drive through Lynchburg earlier in the morning so they knew that we were on our way. As it turns out when looking at the sign in log we were the most recent of a long list of family members that made the drive over the past week. Driving up to the small collection of buildings on Bear Mountain I could feel the connection with the place and the people there… it really is an indescribable feeling.

We were greeted warmly upon our arrival and after paying the modest admission fee we were shown to the next room where we watched a brief video about the history of our people. Given her recent passing, hearing Chief Sharon Bryant's voice was both soothing knowing that her legacy lives on and also heartbreaking knowing all that she would have been able to accomplish if given more time.

Upon the conclusion of the movie, we all got up and walked into the next room to learn as much as we could during our visit. Holding my son as I walked in, I was motivated even more to find the documents and information needed to become a member of the Monacan Nation. While looking around I was able to find a few more pieces of information for my research and I was able to speak with the woman who originally greeted us about what needed to be done.

Even though the museum only consisted of three rooms we spent well over an hour looking around, talking, and learning about this part of our family history and heritage. After making sure it was okay to walk around and take pictures, we went next door to the Indian Mission School. Given the years that it was used there is a good possibility that there were a few ancestors that received their education within those walls. It is amazing to think that the school was used until the 1960's.

From within that small school house, one can look out the window and see the Episcopal Church just across a small creek. A central part of the community, we walked over to the church to take a closer look and when we turned the corner and approached the front entrance, a kaleidoscope of butterflies floated across the bridge laced clearing between the buildings and converged on the flowering bushes in front of us.

As we walked away, the butterflies scattered into the wind. I am not usually one to think along these lines but I felt at that moment that was the way our ancestors were welcoming us back. It didn't look or feel as though it was just a coincidence.

Feeling both drained and energized, we got back in the car and drove up the road to another place I had only seen in pictures. Thankfully, we noticed the small sign along the side of the road and just a few minutes later I found myself standing in front of the final resting place for many of my ancestors. Within the lines of the single headstone at the front of the cemetery, many of my family surnames can be found... Redcross, Terry, Beverly, and Johns.

Behind this headstone are the graves marked with anonymous stones. All recognized as individuals but buried as a people. It was the most moving part of the journey and gave me a lot to think about as we drove back through the mountains. Hopefully the next time I am able to visit will be as a member of the tribe and not just as a visitor.

A Surprising Stay

A few days into our trip we packed up the car and headed slightly north to Lexington, the second stop of our Virginia tour. The Red Roof Inn in Troutville served its purpose but it was far from an excellent place to stay… stayed in worse and stayed in better. With the change we knew that we would be staying at the Hampton Inn which we thought would be a step up from where we were. What we didn't expect was how big that step would turn out to be… the historic Hampton Inn in Lexington (main building built in 1820) was quite the surprise.

During our stay there we ventured off to a few other locations (i.e. Natural Bridge and Bear Mountain) but also took advantage of both the amenities and architecture at the hotel as well as the close proximity (five minute walk) to the heart of Lexington. By the way, I highly recommend the Southern Inn and Bistro On Main for dinner. Best meals, by far, during the trip.

On our final morning before driving across the Commonwealth, we took advantage of the loose schedule and spent some time at the Stonewall Jackson House which proved to be a fascinating glimpse into the complicated (and some would say conflicted) life of the Confederate general. It is one thing to read a book or watch a movie about him like "Gods and Generals" but it is a different experience and perspective when walking through his home.

From the museum we walked across the street and did something that I haven't done in some time (I actually can't remember the last time)… we went for a carriage ride around town. Much like bus tours we had experienced in the past, this was a great way to get an overview of the town and take in as much as possible with the time that we had. In addition to the slow ride past many of the historic houses and buildings up and down the streets we also passed many of the buildings which are part of Washington & Lee University.

As we made the final turn to return to our original departure point near the Visitor's Center I could see the foreboding buildings of VMI making their presence known in the distance. And as the fortress like structure came into view we passed the resting place of one of the former instructors… Stonewall Jackson.

Back at the car as my family stretched for one last time, I ducked into the Rockbridge County Historical Society. While not as fruitful as I was hoping, it was a good conversation nevertheless and I was able to walk out of the small building with a few new contacts in the area for further research inquiries. With our feet beginning to throb we welcomed the long drive although there was a little letdown having to leave these counties to which we are so closely tied. So long Botetourt, Rockbridge, and Amherst Counties. We will be back again soon!

Virginia Discoveries

Not long after the reunion dinner started, those of us in attendance were presented with new genealogical information regarding our family history. This was a revelation to many of those in attendance and I was rather eager to see this new research that was being brought to our attention. Within the blue folder, in front of the directory of those in attendance that weekend, there were two pages (206-207) copied from Joan Wheeler LaGrone's book "Chronicles of a Nation" detailing the history of the original family surname.

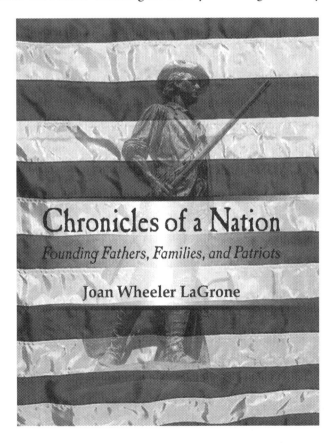

While many saw this as an expansion of the family tree, when I read through the short excerpt I realized it was more like a collection of leaves that had fallen to the ground. We know which tree they came from but we can't be certain yet as to from which branch they fell. However, it is great information to have and while I was familiar with the New Jersey connection (they retained a surname that more closely resembles the original), I was unfamiliar with the history of the surname as well as the more recent Civil War era stories that were relayed in the book.

While that new information satisfied the curiosity of many, there were many other opportunities throughout our journey across the commonwealth that really provided additional color to the leaves in our tree. Many of these revelations occurred during a conversation I had with a Monacan woman at the living history exhibit at Natural Bridge. It was from this conversation that I learned of John Redcross's participation at the Battle of Yorktown during the Revolutionary War. While I previously knew of his general service and the company to which he belonged, I was unfamiliar with his participation at this celebrated victory.

This conversation also put some pieces together for me as I found out that many Monacan families moved to Eagle Rock at the same time as my ancestors. I was always curious as to why they chose to move there and this provided me with a logical explanation… they were part of a group that moved rather than as an individual family. Finally, when discussing additional details regarding the documents needed to prove our ancestral claims, she provided additional guidance as to what documents to use and where we should look for other supporting information. Thankfully, we already have many of the documents that were discussed.

The day after our time at Natural Bridge, we traveled to the Monacan Indian Museum in Amherst County. Once again, the woman there to greet us was warm, inviting, and seemed genuinely excited to discuss our pursuit of membership in the tribe. In addition to the advice that was generously bestowed upon us (and my Aunt a few days prior), I came across a book on display in one of the cabinets that offered a couple of pieces of missing information… the death dates for Preston Johns and his wife Louisa Terry (my third great grandmother – mother of Marcellias Nicholas Love).

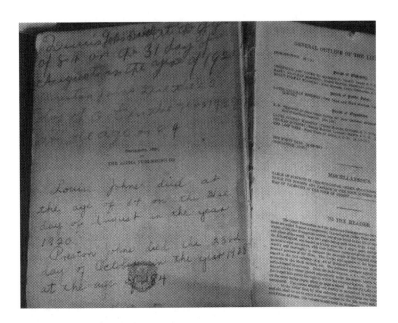

With so much new information, advice, and connections made I am definitely looking forward to putting a few more pieces together as well as filling in the application I picked up for tribal membership. While this entire trip was a revelation of place, these moments were a revelation of knowledge. All of these things – people, places, events, information, connections, etc. – make up who we are and I am looking forward to retelling this story to everyone but most especially my son.

Keeping In Touch

After the reunion, I was determined to improve my communication with family members both nearby and far away. After all, there is only so much that I can do with regard to genealogy and it is always best to be in communication with numerous family members trying to fill in the different pieces rather than all of use trying to find all of the answers on our own. Additionally, we all have access to different documents, photos, and stories that we should be sharing with one another. That might have been the biggest takeaway from the family gathering... there is so much that we all possess and it would be nice for us all to have access to those pieces of the picture and leaves of the tree.

While in the past this would have been a more exaggerated process full of letters and a lot of postage. That isn't the reality in which we live today. While there are some that still require the letters, phone calls, and face to face meetings, most can be accomplished through email and social media. Thankfully, there has already been a group formed on Facebook to help facilitate those communications and I have been able to connect with those who were in attendance as well as those who were unable to make it.

Sometimes it is also these simple things that get other family members interest in family history. I have been able to connect with many family members, some of whom to which I have not previously spoken, based on the simple fact that they want to learn more about the family. In other instances, different stories have been shared... some I have heard before while others are completely new to me. I doubt that the correspondences would have come as easily through any other means other than Facebook or email.

Of course, there are a lot more stories that have yet to be told and information that hasn't as of yet been shared but the lines of communication are open and I am looking forward to collecting and sharing these new tidbits with the rest of the family. So, the reunion turned out to last much longer than the two days in Virginia, and I expect it to continue until we are able to get together again five years from now... we should have a much more colorful and complete tree by then.

Planning For 2020

Five years seems a long way off but if it goes by as fast as the last half decade it won't be long before we are all, once again, heading down to Virginia for another reunion. Recently I have been thinking about different things to include the next time around and what I would like to see organized by the next time we get together. Some of these things are general ideas while others are specific items I want to finally check off my list.

Bear in mind, these are things that I hope to do in order to enhance or build upon the fantastic work that has already been done in previous years. We are a big family and it is similar to herding chickens when it comes to getting us all together. Each reunion, from what I have heard since I have only been to two, has been a great experience for all in attendance and a tremendous success overall. Like putting the pieces together in the family tree, I hope to build upon what has already been done.

So, let's start with the general, yet specific, things that I hope we are able to arrange. The first big one is a project that I am not spearheading (but I will be happy to assist) which is getting the family tree (all branches) loaded onto a website where all family members will have access and can notify us of any updates. This will also be a great place where documents and pictures can be shared and enjoyed by all. I really hope to see this up and running well before the next reunion.

Personally, I hope to coordinate tours of some of the towns and places where our family once (and still does in certain instances) lived. This was a great experience when we walked around these places over the summer and I hope to have a larger group next time around. Additionally, I hope to have a listing of the local cemeteries where we can find our cousins, grandparents, great grandparents, aunts, uncles, etc. Hopefully, we can add a few names to this list as well before the next reunion. Lastly, it would be nice to have access to the local records offices so that we can have basically a group research project. It should be much more efficient with each of us searching for different pieces and putting them together at the end of the day.

Of course, there are also numerous goals that I hope to reach by the time we meet again. First and foremost are the applications to the Sons of the American Revolution and the Monacan Indian Nation. The former is purely a formality as we have more than enough documentation to satisfy the membership requirements. The latter is proving to be more difficult as specific documents need to be found in order to prove lineage. It is not an impossible task just a tedious one. However, it will all be worth it in the end.

In addition to the above, I hope to secure some donations for the raffle and coordinate what I hope will be some fun activities. As I think about it, Genealogy Jeopardy or Six Degrees of Family History could be interesting games to play. Pursuing raffle items could be interesting as well given that there are a variety of books that pertain to our family history, memberships and application fees that would be great auction items, as well as prints and other items that would be great to create (although I don't think we could do better than the quilt that was raffled off this time around).

I am also curious to pursue various possible partnerships. It would be great to partner with a site like ancestry.com to add another dimension to the gathering. I hope to have mutually beneficial things like this coordinated so that we get some great insights into the family research while they (ancestry or some other site/group) have a perfect opportunity for a case study. After all, many of us are on ancestry already and can tell our family story through the leaves on the trees and the items that we have personally uploaded.

In the end, the most important thing for me to do personally is to keep working on the family history. Not just searching for and collecting the facts, documents, and photos but telling the stories of the family. The stories are certainly plentiful, it is just a matter of sitting down and recording the family history.

A Genealogist's Perspective

Unintentional Intentional Errors

Every once in a while I will receive a message through my Ancestry.com account regarding some of the information in my family tree. Sometimes it is about documents, photos, or certain details that I have discovered elsewhere and uploaded to the website which I am happy to share and discuss with anyone who contacts me… you never know how you might be related. However, most of the time, the questions and corrections are regarding the very tips of the limbs that I have yet to fully research. In these instances I reply letting them know that the research has yet to be done and the information is stemming from scant documents that have been uncovered. This is usually followed by an invitation to share any information they might have on that individual or, as has been the case a few times, the correct name that should be inscribed on that leaf.

This all comes down to how each of us use Ancestry as a genealogical research tool. While many people refuse to enter information in their tree until they have verified the content, I prefer to use the website to both record known facts and figures but also theorize as to those names that may consist of the next generation. Sometimes it can be stemming from information culled from documents and other times it is a much more general estimation given the age of children, where subsequent generations lived, and sometimes the information that has been passed down in the family.

Even the most basic of estimations have sometimes led to the information that I have been looking for. Many times I have entered the surname and approximate year of birth to find only a handful of possible people who could fit into my tree. After looking at all the records available, I was able to not only find the right name but verify that, yes, they are my ancestor. All it takes is that small detail and a little bit of deduction in order to begin chipping away at that wall. This is the process that has worked for me and has kept me somewhat organized in my research thought process over the years.

Of course, with this being my process it leaves a number of assumptions wilting under the sun on the end of the branch until I am able to make the time to prune them but I know that the information is there and I don't have to worry about retracing some of my steps over and over again when I find the rare moments to search for that next generation. Again, while not a process for everyone, it is the one that has worked best for me so far. Now if I could only be so organized with all the photos, documents, and notes cluttering my office.

Exploring The New Ancestry

It has now been some time since I updated my ancestry.com account to the new format. I was a little hesitant to do so as I felt I was just starting to really get a handle on the old site. Besides, what would I really get out of the new format if I wasn't able to find everything that I wanted? But, not having the time that I used to have to comb through the digital volumes that I once had and getting tired of the constant requests to upgrade, I finally just decided to go ahead and make the change. After all, the constant promotions promised an enhanced experience far superior to the supposedly antiquated site that I had been using so let's see what all the fuss is about.

Well… there isn't much difference between the old site and the new one. At least, nothing significant that I have noticed in my occasional browsing through files, searching for documents, and skimming across the vast family tree that I have constructed. While I can clearly see the shiny new layer of digital shellac, where is the revolutionary change in functionality? It was really a letdown when the new site was laid out before me on the computer screen.

With that said, there is one minor feature that I particularly enjoy but it isn't anything that will rock the genealogy world. While I am constantly cognizant of the world and sometimes local events that took place during the lifetime of my ancestor, ancestry now has those historical reminders integrated into each family member's timeline. And I have to admit that it is helpful from time to time having those simple reminders clearly displayed on the screen.

Other than that, I haven't come across anything that is making things easier or more interesting… of course, my family history is already deeply fascinating to me so it would be hard to enhance that. At the same time, as the updates were occurring, ancestry.com kept making more and more collections available for search… these have been more useful than the prettier packaging that the website is now offering. This is what made me think, what if they put their money and effort into making more documents available rather than redesigning the website? How much more data would we all have access to? What could we have already discovered?

That is, first and foremost, where the focus should always be not on how fancy the site looks but what information the site contains. So I ask ancestry.com to spend those membership dollars on data not on spit and polish. After all, the reason why we give you our hard earned money is to learn more about our family not the fanciness of the page framing the digital document.

Anyone Know Of A Good AA Group Around Here?

Despite our frequent warnings, this past week my wife and I had a friend of ours finally take the plunge and get onto ancestry.com. Since then we have noticed a significant increase in their time spent online sometimes going well past midnight. Of course, this is one of the early warning signs and my wife finally got to the point that she had to ask the question that was also floating around in the empty space of my mind, "Are you getting too addicted already?!?!"

We ask because we are and, if need be, we will have an intervention. We know the signs all too well and we know the constant pull that the website has during all hours of the day and night. We are Ancestry Addicts and we are proud of it.

Unfortunately, I don't think our friend really knows what they are getting themselves into. It starts with a small hit and a high that is just enough to make you want more. Soon it is never enough and you are spending hours at a time on the computer without even knowing it. One night you get on for a quick search at 10:00 PM and before you know it the light peers through the blinds and it's time for breakfast.

And, if that wasn't bad enough, it gets worse. Soon your reaching out to relatives you haven't spoken to in years grilling them for more details about a cousin you just discovered or an Aunt that caused a ruckus in her neighborhood in 1924 because she didn't care for the art deco designs. That's when you find that only an addict knows how to satisfy an addict. The rest of the world doesn't care if your great great grand pappy had the grandest outhouse in the county and before you started chasing the genealogical dragon you didn't care either.

There really is no end to the vicious cycle of research and discovery and I wouldn't have it any other way. I am a heritage hoarder and an ancestry addict and I'm darn proud of that fact. I am finding out who I am by finding the people that made my family what it is today. I will continue to search and I will always look for new places to explore. And while I am looking elsewhere I will continue to return to the tree and, occasionally, partake in some of the good stuff, the easy highs, that come about when a new leaf appears and taunts me with its shimmy.

Yeah, I have problems but I can't stop to think about that now, I have more work to do and files to organize. Of course, when I have a minute here or there, I might see if there are any good Ancestry Anonymous groups out there. It's always better when you get high with others.

From Genealogy To Freemasonry To Religion: A LinkedIn Group Conversation

* *

Well, I should have expected it but I posted a discussion on LinkedIn with the hope that people would keep to the topic of the group and the intention of the post. Basically, I had taken a post from a few days ago regarding the tour that I gave to a perspective candidate on Tuesday night and how we shared a commonality in our journey to Freemasonry. Our similar stories revolved around the genealogy that we had done on our respective families. With that in mind, I thought that those in the various genealogy groups that I am in would appreciate this coincidence. I also wanted the post to serve as an introduction to masonic records as a valuable genealogical tool.

Thankfully, there were a few people, masons and non-masons alike, which read this post and contributed to the discussion in the way that it was intended. However, there were others that proved to me that the anti-masonic movement is still alive and well (and now on LinkedIn). My favorite fallacy was posted by a supposed former Brother who wrote the following:

> Freemasons Hall in London is very helpful with enquiries about masonic ancestors. It is indeed a fascinating subject.
>
> However, having myself been Master of four lodges including one in the Antient and Accepted Rite, I concluded that Freemasonry is in fact a major perpetrator of heretical ideas, notably indifferentism, pelagianism and relativism or modernism. These heresies, pushed to their logical conclusion, deny God, and this is what Freemasonry, despite apparent assertions in its ritual to the contrary, also does.

Further down in the discussion I found the following comment:

I suggest that all should read "deadly deception" and find out the true background of masonry - i havebhad the opportunity to denounce all 33 rd degrees and curses over me (unknowingly) by two grandfathers - an uncle and my father .... I agree this forum is for Genealogy NOT masonry!

Please do not write me back - i have 14 books on masonry and breaking free from it! I have studied for years as a born again spirit filled Christian.

So, if I said that I have 15 books on Christianity and have proven all aspects of the New Testament to be false, does that make me an expert? According to this comment it does. But, per her request, I am not writing her back (this essay doesn't count). All I can say is that it is a shame that such a great genealogical resource is ignored because some people chose to believe in the dark propaganda which casts an unfavorable light on many of their own ancestors. Masonry is part of my genealogy and I am proud to carry on this tradition.

"We" Is One Word Not Two Letters

Throughout our travels, no matter where we have gone, every place has had one thing in common... they are all a part of this great country which my family has called home from the very beginning of this nation's founding and has fought for the rights and freedoms for which our flag flies. Once I saw the flag hanging in front of the Asa Packer Mansion in Jim Thorpe I was struck by the reminder that there is more than just a grand structure looking over this small mountain town in the Poconos. And if we pay attention to the world around us we can easily see the tactile representation of our country's founding ideals in the 13 stripes and 50 stars.

Independence Day is not a time of sales and pyrotechnics. Today is a time of pride for every person that has the privilege to call themselves an American. Regardless of our own political opinions and our feelings about whether the government has done something right or wrong, this is a time of unity under one flag that shines brighter than any spark in the sky.

This is a time to remember and honor the sacrifices made not only by those who have fought for and fought to defend liberty but also a time to honor those who chose to come to the United States and make this country their home. It is a time to remember our heritage both as individual families and a nation as a whole. This is a day to reflect on how we honor our ancestors in our own lives.

We must consider what this nation stands for and the rights that we have been granted by G-d and country. We must hold fast to ensure the rights and freedoms of every person during this time of great change in which we live. It is our duty and our responsibility to uphold the rights and freedoms of others regardless of whether we personally partake in those liberties. So long as we hold in our hearts the fact that rights are not optional we can keep the history, memory, and ideals of this nation's founding alive and ensure that our nation will continue to thrive.

Let your neighbor know, let the world know, that we are one nation and our flag hangs ever-present not as a representation of the government but as a symbol of a united people. Today we are not two parties, we are one people. We are not a country of religious strife; we are one nation under G-d. We are Americans and we are proud of our history.

What Does Your Last Name Mean To You?

Having spent countless hours working on my family genealogy I am always reevaluating what my name really means to me. What does it mean to my family? What weight does it carry and how do the actions and experiences of our ancestors influence who we are today?

It was with these thoughts and questions running through my mind that I watched the documentary "Hitler's Children". If you never thought about how the actions of your ancestors influence who you are this is the movie you need to watch. It demonstrates how powerful our name is in shaping who we are and how our genealogy can shape our lives.

The documentary explores the lives of the descendants of prominent Nazi's and how they cope with the burden of the past. For those who live with the last names of Himmler, Frank, Goering, Hoess their name ties them with genocide. They have a direct connection to the death camps; their family legacy is that of extermination. While some families may have skeletons, these people have monsters in their closet.

It is an interesting contradiction to the emotional ties that many people have and the associations that their last names carry. One's surname can invoke prominent thoughts of their ancestry and a strong bond with their heritage: Irish, English, Italian, Spanish, Native American, Eastern European, Asian and even many positive German connections. Imagine the absence of pride; think of the horror of being so closely tied to the abominations of the Nazi regime.

All of the descendants in this film wrestle with knowing. There is no mystery. They know their name and the power it carries. They know the terror that their name still invokes in the victims, survivors, and decedents of the Holocaust. I can't fathom the immense burden they these people live with every day of their lives... I can't grasp the fear of having some part of those monsters inside me. The strength that these people have is immeasurable. These people are the generation that offers hope and they need to be remembered as much as their heinous ancestors.

I take pride in the names and generations of my family. I accept the good and the bad. Regardless, I look forward to knowing more about the people in my tree, the lives they lived, and the places from which we came. I don't know if I would be able to handle knowing of such monsters in my family's past and knowing the same tainted blood was running through my veins. I am German; I am Irish; I am Native American; I am English; I am many things, all of which I am proud.

Watch and think about your own family. Appreciate what you have and look to find out more. Whether you realize it or not, your name is a big part of what makes you who you are and the more you know about it the more you will find out about yourself.

Only A Small Part Of The Story

Recently, TLC brought back the show "Who Do You Think You Are?" My wife and I enjoy watching the weekly episodes and learning about the interesting family histories that some celebrities are willing to share with the world. Seeing the reactions on the faces of those people can also be just as intriguing as we both know that feeling well of when something unexpected is discovered.

However, for me there has always been something missing. One of the fascinating aspects of genealogy for me has been the vastly different stories that our ancestors have. Many times, if you trace enough lines, you can find your ancestors in opposition whether it may be north against south, Indian versus settler, or some other means of conflict. These are the stories that shape us.

We are shaped by all our ancestors and the lives that each one of them lived both the remarkable and the ordinary. Sometimes it is more about the place rather than the person that adds depth and understanding. For instance, knowing that one of my ancestors came from the Alsace Lorraine region in France but considered himself and was recognized upon immigration as German adds an interesting complexity to my ancestor's life and to our family history.

Do we consider ourselves only German as our ancestor did or do we more accurately consider ourselves both? This is the kind of interesting internal question that really doesn't have an answer as it is nearly impossible to balance the considerations from an ancestor's life and how they viewed themselves with the facts that shaped the world around them. This is the type of question that is frequently missing from the series.

During each episode the story of discovery is fascinating but it is by no means an accurate depiction of the process. Anyone who has done any kind of in depth genealogy understands the time and energy it takes to sometimes find just one item. Generation after generation the tedious process repeats until finally, after countless cycles the leaves of the tree begin to come into focus.

There are times when information is readily available, especially with the constantly expanding digital databases like ancestry.com, but that is still not the norm as many records remain confined to paper or microfilm. When you have to sort through piles of paper and reels of film in order to find a single document you have a much deeper appreciation of your heritage and you hold fast to the knowledge that you had to earn. It was not given to you in front of a camera; you had to work for the information, you had to sweat to find out who you are.

That is what is missing from this show. It is not about being handed your family history, it is about earning your heritage and connecting with your ancestors. That is how you truly find out who you are.

Finding Your Roots vs. Who Do You Think You Are?

When talking about genealogy with people it is common for the conversation to touch upon the show "Who Do You Think You Are?" Over the years, all different kinds of people have watched the show regardless of their interest level in genealogy as a whole or their own family tree… they usually watch because they are a fan of some actor, actress, or athlete and want to learn a little more about them. More often than not, this leads them to jump to the conclusion of "I wish I had stories like that in my family tree."

The people I have spoken with make that determination that those types of stories do not exist in their tree mostly because the show focuses on a single line in that celebrity's genealogy. I guess you could say that is the one thing that many of us familiar with genealogy have a problem with when it comes to the show "Who Do You Think You Are?" It is for this reason that I tend to pay closer attention to and enjoy "Finding Your Roots" a little more than the main stream counterpart.

Like any PBS show, "Finding Your Roots" isn't as well-known but it takes a much more interesting and broader look at the ancestry of celebrities (of all kinds not just main stream). During the course of an episode, three family trees are analyzed with a common thread running between the three stars. Sometimes it can be as broad as overcoming adversity while other times it is tied to a specific event such as the roles their ancestors played in the Civil War.

While that is one difference (one vs. three) the other, more important and more interesting differentiator is the fact that the latter of the two shows looks at the family tree as a whole not just a singular line (or two). From my own experience, I know that this is the most interesting part of genealogy as you never know what names, places, and events may be adding color to the individual leaves. After all, we are the culmination of all these people who played, for the most part, equal roles in determining the family story and making us who we are.

"Who Do You Think You Are" may have the bigger audience, interesting locations, and larger budget, "Finding Your Roots" brings us closer to the interesting realities of doing genealogical research. Furthermore, the latter show also explores the use of DNA in discovering the mix of places, races, and heritage that exists within all of us. This is why my preference is quite clear but, in the end, taking a look at the sponsorship, Ancestry.com wins no matter which show you prefer.

Continuing The Debate: Genealogy Roadshow Returns

I previously wrote about the preferences that many of us have for Finding Your Roots or Who Do You Think You Are? This lead to a tremendous discussion on LinkedIn (in a few groups) about the pros and cons of each and, in many instances, what is missing from each show. Keep in in mind that all of those who participated in this back and forth have been researching their own family history and so many of the sticking points surrounded the lack of process demonstrated in each program.

Another prevalent point made was of the disconnect from those of us actually doing the work. Many of the participants in each of these shows are, for the most part, along for the ride without actually doing the work themselves. We all know the hours, days, weeks, years that this journey takes to make the kind of progress depicted in a 60 minute program. So the back and forth continued regarding these two current programs with a few references made to other shows that were no longer on the air.

One show that was brought up for both its positive qualities and because of the things that it lacks was Genealogy Roadshow. Many of us had seen the program when it was on but many others completely missed it and wondered what it was about. We didn't discuss it much further than that because, at the time, it was not currently showing and none of us expected to see it return to PBS. Honestly, the conversation continued and I once again completely forgot about the short lived series until a few weeks ago when I got a press release in my email.

Simply put, Genealogy Roadshow is back! In the end, all genealogy shows are going to have faults but the important thing is that they are on the television and people are slowly becoming exposed to the importance of knowing who they are and where they come from. I am sure there will be continued debate on this subject.

The Lost Genealogy Show

In a recent discussion on LinkedIn there was another genealogy program brought to my attention. After reading the back and forth around the pros and cons of the mainstream programs (i.e. Who Do You Think You Are?, Finding Your Roots, and Genealogy Roadshow) I was interested to watch a YouTube video to see if this new program (pilot actually) did a better job especially with regard to process. Honestly, my expectations were not very high as I have seen numerous attempts at programs online but I figured that I would give it a shot.

While the intro to "Legend Seekers" leaves a little something to be desired the program itself is excellent. It is kind of the best of all worlds in that it is not reliant upon celebrity and it does not overburden itself with trying to take too broad a view of a family tree. Rather, the focus of the program is on a singular event in the history of a regular family. It is the kind of thing that all of us immersed in our own family history do on a regular basis just in a more condensed and presentable format.

While there is a lot that is left on the floor with regard to the process, there is still much more information regarding the resources that are available for people to conduct their own research and to whom they can turn to find the information that they are seeking. There are also tips and additional information to assist the viewer in their own research particularly regarding Census records and the wealth of information that can be found in cemeteries. While many of us who have been doing this for a while know this information it is always worth being reminded and it is of huge value to those who may just be getting started.

The program also shows the slight bumps and detours that we all run into. However, similar to mine and many other experiences that I have read, persistence can sometimes pay off as it did in the search for the Lively family in this episode. This is both an interesting and motivating program for those who are interested in researching their own family.

With all of that said, I do have one rather large problem with the program… this is the only episode that was made due to the lack of funding and not having been picked up for a full season. There are so many stories out there in every family that it would be great to see the stories that, for the most part, remain untold. Heck, I can think of a half dozen in my own family (a few of which have previously been mentioned) that I would like to see produced in this manner. Hopefully, sometime in the future, the show will return and give us a better example of what the real process is like… I would much rather spend the time watching more episodes of this rather than the aforementioned mainstream programs.

About the Author

Sean M. Teaford has gained a reputation as a talented poet, thorough researcher, and insightful essayist with honest images that remain with the reader long after the page has been turned. Over the past fifteen years, Sean has published over a hundred poems and over a thousand online articles. Many recent articles center on his own family history the depth and breadth of which spans countless generations and geographies.

Over the past decade, Sean has authored four poetry collections and currently maintains a daily blog, Time To Keep It Simple, which has served as a record of his life as a traveler, writer, genealogist, photographer, Rotarian, Mason, convert to Judaism, and, most importantly, as a husband and new father. Additionally, Sean has contributed to various international publications.

In addition to serving as an editor for a variety of literary publications, including the Endicott Review and Mad Poets Review, he has coordinated numerous poetry readings across the Northeast and has been a featured speaker in the Boston and Philadelphia areas. Sean received a M.F.A. in Creative Writing from Rosemont College and a B.A. in English from Endicott College.

A public relations account executive, Sean lives in Morgantown, Pennsylvania with his wife and son.

Printed in the United States
By Bookmasters